The College Student's Guide to Understanding the DSM-5

A summarized format to understanding DSM-5 Disorders

Maria Shkreli, LMHC

This guide contains summarized information relating to mental health. It is not intended to replace medical advice and should not be used to supplement mental health care. The information provided is a summarization and comparison of similarities of disorders to be used as a quick reference guide for individuals studying in the mental health field. All efforts have been made to ensure the accuracy of the information provided. Both publisher and author disclaim any liability for any methods applied or suggested in this guide.

First edition: October 2018

ISBN - 13: 978-0-692-04072-0

Printed in the United States of America.

Contents

Contents

For Christopher and Nicolette

About the Author

Maria Shkreli is a licensed mental health therapist in Pleasantville, New York. She received her master's degree in mental health counseling and marriage and family therapy from Long Island University and Certification in Cognitive Behavior Therapy.

She has extensive work experience in both the private and public sectors. Maria works with individuals, adolescents, teens, couples and families seeking treatment to address anxiety, family conflict, communication issues, couples issues, and emotional difficulties.

Maria is the author of the following books (published by Twentynine Publishing):

- *The Simplified NCMHCE Study Guide: A simplified format to understanding DSM-5 Disorders, Theatrical Orientations and Assessments*
- *The College Student's Guide to Understanding the DSM-5*
- *Help! My Anxious Middle Schooler*
- *I am "Bully"*

Chapter 1

Introduction

Congratulations on purchasing your new study guide. Many times, students are overwhelmed with too much information and, the ability to learn the information becomes difficult. This guide is written in a format that will assist you in understanding the information needed for the psychology courses you'll take in college.

My goal in writing this guide is to cover and compare the differences and similarities between various DSM-5 disorders, and to provide short cases and worksheets for you to test your understanding of DSM-5 disorders.

This guide is also useful for students who are preparing for tests and unsure of their understanding of disorders. The simple format will assist you in learning the material needed to learn DSM-5 disorders and increase your knowledge and understanding of material to pass your exams.

Remember, this guide is not the full DSM-5 criteria. It contains brief references of disorders in a format intended to help you recognize similarities and differences, test your knowledge, use as a quick reference, and for those who want to brush up one last time before tests.

Thank you for your purchase, and the best of luck to you.

Sincerely,

Maria Shkreli, LMHC

The College Student's Guide to Understanding the DSM-5

Test-Taking Tips

Preparing for an exam can be overwhelming and confusing. How do I study, what material do I need, and where do I find it? Try to avoid the "should have/could have" thinking on the exam, as this will guarantee you a fail. A case is presented to you, questions are asked, and possible answers are provided. Stay FOCUSED in the now. So, what to do: Know the DSM-5.

Practice tests! They really help! They really work! Each time you take one, the grade will change. (Take a break in between to determine where you stand.) *Carefully* read the questions and answers in the exam. Some of the answers are found in the case. Be aware of "could be this/might be that" thinking – it's distracting. When you start looking at the question disparately, answers may not be so clear.

When do I start my study plan?
It depends on your exam date. If you are studying 5 hours a week, then your start date might be 2 weeks before your test date. This, of course, will vary for each individual.

Make a study plan:
Time and place you will study
Plan out what you will study – how many and which disorders will you study at each study appointment

Make a list of your disorder knowledge:
List the disorders you understand, as well as the ones you don't understand
Have the full version of the DSM-5 on hand

Expand your plan:
Decide whether a tutor or study group will help your studying
Look into videos/YouTube/psychology sites

Test readiness:
Rate your readiness based on your first practice test results. Spread out your future practice retakes at least one week apart so that you can monitor your strengths and weaknesses. This one-week period will give you time to focus on studying.

Your mindset:
Check in with yourself – are you over-studying, becoming anxious, not motivated? If you answered yes, think about slowing down. **Don't rush.**

Important:
Focus. **Don't over-study – there is evidence that over-studying may reduce your pass rate.**

In the next few chapters, you will find summarized DSM-5 disorders. You will also find case studies that are short and simple to work on, to help engage your thinking as a therapist.

The Guide's chapters include mention of theoretical orientation used by therapists to conceptualize their clients and the presenting issues. The specific theoretical orientation a therapist may use will vary, depending on the client's problem and the therapist's area of expertise. As you progress in your studies, you will learn about assessments and theoretical orientation.

The answers are provided in short form to challenge your understanding of the disorders.

First, before you begin, test your knowledge and understanding by completing the following cases prior to reading the disorders.

Joshua and Jorie have been married for nine years. They have two kids, ages seven and five. Jorie is a stay-at-home mom, and Joshua is the Vice President of a large company. Joshua's job requires him to travel once a month. Since both kids are in school, Jorie has been spending more time on hobbies she enjoys, going to the gym, and occasionally having lunch dates with the other moms.

Joshua has had struggles in his relationship with Jorie for several years, and lately he's noticed that her behavior has gotten worse. Jorie is drinking more, and her behavior hasn't been pleasant. Jorie has been accusing Joshua of cheating on her, and tells him that if he ever leaves her, she'll kill herself. She's also distanced her family, because she feels they have mistreated her. She gets angry and depressed, and her self-image is negative. She feels emptiness, seems paranoid, and has constant mood swings. Jorie's impulsivity and excessive spending has added to Joshua's frustration. Joshua feels stressed over her behavior, doesn't know how to handle her mood swings, and is tired of her paranoia and angry outbursts. Joshua has approached her about his concerns, and she simply states that nothing is wrong and accuses him of not being supportive. Joshua convinces Jorie to see you for help, and calls you to tell you about his concerns. Joshua tells you that Jorie hasn't been taking her medication for several weeks. In addition, he mentions that he's noticed Jorie has small cuts on her body and is afraid that Jorie will harm herself.

What is Jorie's presenting problem?

What are the presenting symptoms?

What is the duration?

What is Jorie's behavior?

What is Jorie's diagnosis?

Kyle is a 26-year-old computer programmer at a small company in his hometown. Kyle lives with his girlfriend, Carrie. Carrie moved in with Kyle two months ago, and is starting to wonder if it was the right choice. Carrie is overwhelmed by Kyle's behavior. Last weekend, Kyle spent 15 hours watching TV, detailed his car and brainstormed on how to start his own business. During this time, he flew from idea to idea and could barely keep up with his rapid speech. He was convinced that he could make a million dollars if he had his own company. Then, four days later, Kyle lost interest in his ideas, was exhausted, and felt hopeless. Carrie noticed his behavior change from feeling that he could do anything (although he took no action on these ideas), to being depressed. These moods last from four days of being on top of the world, to a week of being down. More often, Kyle experiences emptiness and sadness, but not often or severe enough to affect his job or social life. Carrie doesn't know how to help Kyle and tells him she wants to attend therapy.

What is Kyle's presenting problem?

What are the presenting symptoms?

What is the duration?

What is Kyle's behavior?

What is Kyle's diagnosis?

Carlos is a 16-year-old high school student. Carlos is almost six feet tall, and very thin. He rarely wears clothes that fit him; usually his pants are too short.

He is on the honor roll, and involved in computer programming club. Carlos doesn't have many friends at school. He experiences anxiety when he's around the other kids. In addition, he tends to miss social cues and offends the other kids in class. He is often suspicious of kids who talk to him, and feels the only reason they want to talk to him is because they want to steal something from him. Carlos's parents are concerned about his lack of friends and call you for an appointment.

What is Carlos's presenting problem?

What are the presenting symptoms?

What is the duration?

What is Carlos's behavior?

What is Carlos's diagnosis?

Disorders

Chapter 2

Acute Stress Disorder
Adjustment Disorder
Post Traumatic Stress Disorder

Recommended theoretical orientation:

Cognitive Behavioral Therapy
Exposure Therapy
Eye Movement Desensitization & Reprocessing Therapy
Family Therapy
Group Therapy
Solution Focused Brief Therapy

The College Student's Guide

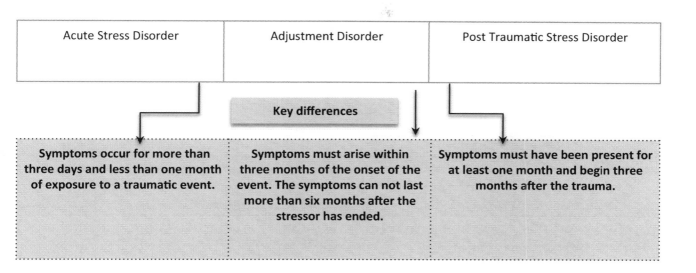

Acute Stress Disorder	Adjustment Disorder	Post Traumatic Stress Disorder

Key differences

Symptoms occur for more than three days and less than one month of exposure to a traumatic event.	**Symptoms must arise within three months of the onset of the event. The symptoms can not last more than six months after the stressor has ended.**	**Symptoms must have been present for at least one month and begin three months after the trauma.**
A traumatic event causes severe anxiety, dissociation, and other symptoms. The individual has three or more of the following symptoms: 1. Intrusion - distressing memories of events 2. Avoidance - memories, feelings, people related to the trauma 3. Arousal - anxiety, irritability, poor concentration, poor sleep **4. Dissociative - being in a daze. Depersonalization/ Derealization** 5. Negative mood - difficulty experiencing happiness	An identifiable stressful event or change in an individual's life causes symptoms, which occur within three months of exposure. One or more symptoms of depressed mood and maladaptive reactions must be present. **No exposure to trauma is experienced.** Symptoms include: 1. Agitation 2. Palpitations 3. Withdrawal 4. Anxiety, stress, and tension 5. Conduct occurrences 6. Physical complaints 7. Impaired social/occupational functioning 8. Depressed mood	Symptoms occur after exposure to an extreme trauma. The trauma elicits intense fear, horror, or helplessness. All of the following symptoms must be present for one month: 1. Re-experiencing of event, flashbacks and nightmares, and physical responses 2. Avoidance of stimuli associated with the trauma, keeping distracted to avoid thinking about the trauma 3. Symptoms of increased arousal - easily startled, on edge, trouble sleeping, trouble concentrating 4. Distressing thoughts, difficulty remembering, loss of interest in activities, feeling distant from people *** PTSD does not experience symptom 4 as Acute Stress Disorder**

Chapter 3

Agoraphobia
Dependent Personality Disorder
Generalized Anxiety Disorder
Panic Disorder
Selective Mutism
Separation Anxiety Disorder
Social Anxiety Disorder

Recommended theoretical orientation:

Behavioral Therapy
Cognitive Behavioral Therapy
Group Therapy
Exposure Therapy
Family Therapy
Interpersonal Therapy
Psychodynamic
Psychotherapy

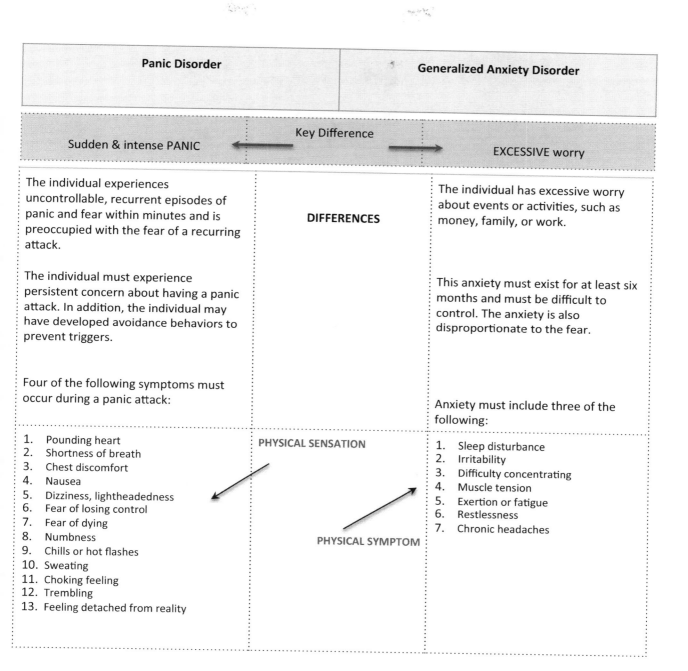

Panic Disorder	Generalized Anxiety Disorder
Sudden & intense PANIC ← Key Difference →	**EXCESSIVE worry**

Panic Disorder	DIFFERENCES	Generalized Anxiety Disorder
The individual experiences uncontrollable, recurrent episodes of panic and fear within minutes and is preoccupied with the fear of a recurring attack. The individual must experience persistent concern about having a panic attack. In addition, the individual may have developed avoidance behaviors to prevent triggers. Four of the following symptoms must occur during a panic attack:	**DIFFERENCES**	The individual has excessive worry about events or activities, such as money, family, or work. This anxiety must exist for at least six months and must be difficult to control. The anxiety is also disproportionate to the fear. Anxiety must include three of the following:
1. Pounding heart 2. Shortness of breath 3. Chest discomfort 4. Nausea 5. Dizziness, lightheadedness 6. Fear of losing control 7. Fear of dying 8. Numbness 9. Chills or hot flashes 10. Sweating 11. Choking feeling 12. Trembling 13. Feeling detached from reality	PHYSICAL SENSATION PHYSICAL SYMPTOM	1. Sleep disturbance 2. Irritability 3. Difficulty concentrating 4. Muscle tension 5. Exertion or fatigue 6. Restlessness 7. Chronic headaches

Separation Anxiety Disorder	Dependent Personality Disorder	Social Anxiety Disorder
(Appears in children)	(Adult)	(Appears in mid-teens)
The individual experiences excessive anxiety when separated from an individual to whom they are attached. The child must have symptoms that last for at least four weeks and the onset must occur before the age of 18.	**Persistent dependence on other people - manifests itself by early adulthood.**	**Persistent fear of social situations or a situation when the individual may need to perform.** The fear/anxiety has a negative impact on the individual's life and must be present for at least six months.
Individual will manifest the following symptoms:	Individual will manifest the following symptoms:	Individual will experience distress in the following situations:
1. Extreme distress when separated from home or the attachment figure 2. Persistent fear of being alone 3. Frequent physical complaints while separated from the attachment figure	1. The need to be taken care of 2. Inability to make decisions on their own 3. Relies on others to assume responsibility for their life 4. Relies on the constant advice of others 5. Difficulties with expressing disagreements 6. Fear of separation 7. Feeling of helplessness	1. Meeting other people 2. Easily embarrassed 3. Feeling insecure and out of place 4. Having to speak in public 5. Being the center of attention 6. Being criticized

Agoraphobia	Selective Mutism
(Appears in late adolescence/early adulthood)	(Appears in children)

The individual is anxious about being outside of the home or in open places. **Fear of a PANIC ATTACK occurring when leaving the home, not a fear of people.** Symptoms are present for at least six months:	**A complex childhood anxiety disorder characterized by a child's inability to speak in a social setting when it's appropriate to speak.** Symptoms are present for at least one month:
1. Fear of being outside the home 2. Fear of public transportation 3. Fear of enclosed/open places 4. Fear of inability to escape when needed	1. Doesn't speak when he/she should 2. Lack of speaking gets in the way of school and friendships 3. Doesn't have a speech problem

Chapter 4

Bipolar I Disorder
Bipolar II Disorder
Cyclothymic Disorder
Major Depressive Disorder
Persistent Depressive Disorder (Dysthymia)
Postpartum Depression
Seasonal Affective Disorder

Recommended theoretical orientation:

Cognitive Behavioral Therapy
Dialectical Behavior Therapy
Family Therapy
Interpersonal Therapy
Light Therapy – Light Boxes
Psychotherapy
Psychodynamic

Bipolar I (also known as manic depressive)	Bipolar II
A disorder characterized by episodes of elevated mood, with alternating episodes of depression.	A disorder characterized by a pattern of one or more major depressive episodes and at least one hypomanic episode.
MUST have a manic episode	Never has a manic episode
CAN have a hypomanic episode	**MUST have a hypomanic episode (lasts for four days)**
CAN have a depressive episode	**MUST have a depressive episode**

KEY DIFFERENCES

Bipolar I: Mania is more severe; Bipolar II: Experiences hypomania

Mania	Hypomania
Significantly elevated mood. **Symptoms persistent for most of the day and last at least one week (or less, if hospitalized).**	Depressive episode never severe enough to cause impairment in functioning, or to require hospitalization. **Symptoms last four days.**

Mania
- Excessive talking
- Less need for sleep
- Poor appetite, weight loss
- Aggressive behavior
- Easily distracted
- Flight of ideas
- Inflated self-esteem
- Engages in activities that can have negative consequences

Hypomania
- Inflated self-esteem
- Less need for sleep
- Very talkative
- Racing thoughts
- Excessive talking
- Engages in activities that can have negative consequences

Major Depressive Disorder In Adults	Major Depressive Disorder In Children
A serious mood disorder. Severe symptoms that affect daily activities, how one thinks, how one feels, eating habits, and sleep habits. Individual experiences five or more of the following symptoms for two consecutive weeks: •Loss of interest in activities and/or ability to feel pleasure •Depressed mood •Decrease or increase in appetite (weight gain or loss) •Insomnia (often) or hypersomnia (sleeps excessively) •Feelings of worthlessness/guilt •Loss of energy; fatigue •Thoughts of death •Motor agitation - poor memory and concentration Episodes cause distress and/or social impairment. Episodes do not meet criteria for substance abuse, manic episode, hypomanic episode, schizophrenia, or other psychotic disorders.	Young children will be depressed and/or irritable most of the time. They also lose interest in activities (most of the time) for at least two weeks: •Crankiness and/or irritability •Unusual sadness •Reduced interest in activities, friends •No longer sees things as pleasurable •Changes in weight •Changes in sleep patterns; sluggishness •Inappropriate guilt, harsh on themselves •Extreme case, kids have thoughts of or make attempt at suicide

Persistent Depressive Disorder (formerly known as Dysthymic)	Cyclothymic Disorder (milder form of Bipolar)
This disorder shares symptoms with major depressive and dysthymic disorder. The symptoms are less severe but chronic.	The individual's symptoms alternate between highs and lows of hypomanic and depressive (mild form) and are chronic. Hypomania/depression are present for at least half the time and not more than two consecutive months without symptoms over a two-year period (one for children).
Depressive symptoms are present for two years and for most of each day. Symptoms must be present for at least one year for adolescents and children.	**Symptoms are present for two years in adults, and for at least one year in children/adolescents.**
Two or more of the following: • Low self-esteem • Decreased appetite or overeating • Feeling of hopelessness • Fatigue • Inability to concentrate • Insomnia • Anger/irritability • Sadness • Decrease in productivity	**Depressive symptoms (symptoms can never meet criteria for a major depressive episode):** • Sadness/hopelessness • Irritability • Low self-esteem • Loss of interest in activities • Inability to concentrate • Loneliness • Social withdrawal
Episodes do not meet criteria for major depressive disorder, cyclothymic disorder, manic episode, schizophrenia, or other psychotic disorders.	**Hypomanic symptoms (symptoms can never meet criteria for a hypomanic episode):** • Irritability • Easily distracted • Increased drive • Overeating • Impulsive • More talkative • Racing thoughts

Postpartum Depression	Seasonal Affective Disorder
(specifer within Major Depressive Disorder)	(specifer within Major Depressive Disorder)

A form of depression experienced by women after childbirth. Symptoms can start within the first few weeks of childbirth or months after childbirth. Depressive symptoms, sadness, can interfere with a woman's ability to care for her family and herself. The likelihood of experiencing postpartum depression is higher for women with a history of depression.

A form of depression that occurs at the same time every year. Most common in the fall and early winter and lasting until the spring or summer.

An individual must meet the criteria for major depression coinciding with specific seasons.

Common symptoms include:

- Frequent crying
- Irritability or anxiety
- Loss of interest or pleasure in activities
- Loss of appetite
- Low motivation and energy
- Little interest in the baby
- Weight loss or gain
- Hopelessness, guilty feeling
- Disruption of sleep, too much sleep, not enough sleep

Symptoms must be present for two years

Winter symptoms include:
- Possible weight gain
- Desire to be alone
- Increase in appetite
- Difficulty concentrating
- Headaches
- Irritability and anxiety
- Loss of energy and/or fatigue

Summer symptoms include:
- Decrease in appetite
- Sleep disturbances
- Change in appetite or weight
- Insomnia
- Irritability and anxiety

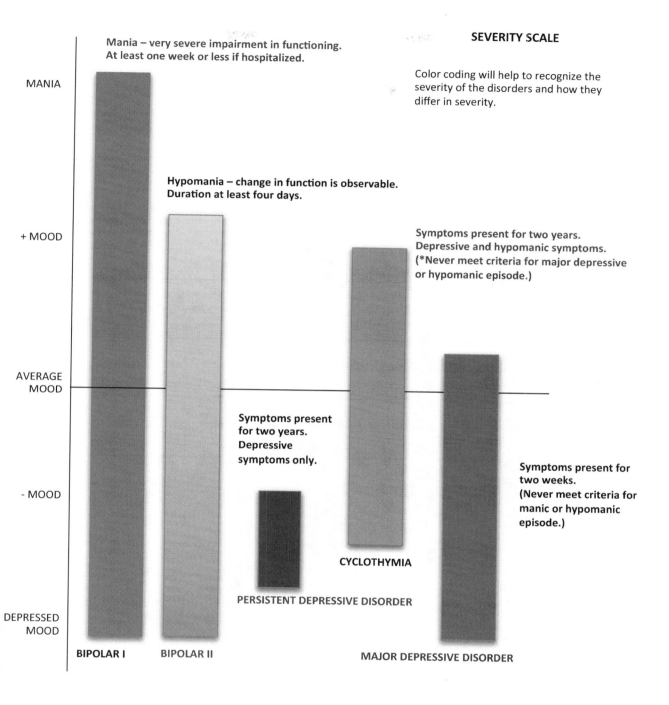

MANIA

Mania – very severe impairment in functioning.
At least one week or less if hospitalized.

SEVERITY SCALE

Color coding will help to recognize the
severity of the disorders and how they
differ in severity.

Hypomania – change in function is observable.
Duration at least four days.

+ MOOD

Symptoms present for two years.
Depressive and hypomanic symptoms.
(*Never meet criteria for major depressive
or hypomanic episode.)

AVERAGE
MOOD

Symptoms present
for two years.
Depressive
symptoms only.

Symptoms present for
two weeks.
(Never meet criteria for
manic or hypomanic
episode.)

- MOOD

CYCLOTHYMIA

PERSISTENT DEPRESSIVE DISORDER

DEPRESSED
MOOD

BIPOLAR I

BIPOLAR II

MAJOR DEPRESSIVE DISORDER

Chapter 5

Borderline Personality Disorder
Histrionic Disorder
Narcissistic Personality Disorder

Recommended theoretical orientation:

Cognitive Behavioral Therapy
Psychotherapy
Dialectical Behavioral Therapy

Borderline Personality Disorder	Histrionic Personality Disorder	Narcissistic Personality Disorder

Key differences

A mental condition – includes impulsive behavior and reckless behavior, unstable relationships and moods. Suffer BRIEF PSYCHOTIC mood swings.	Individual is vulnerable (emotionally) and needs constant praise from people. Inappropriately seductive, manipulative, and flirtatious.	Individual has a significantly inflated sense of self-worth. Lacks empathy, has an arrogant attitude, is envious, and exploits other individuals.
Individual displays a pervasive pattern of instability in affect, impulsivity, instability of social relationships, and self-image. Tends to have "all-or-nothing" thinking.	Individual is excessively emotional and exhibits attention-seeking behavior.	Individual has an extreme preoccupation with self; their distorted thoughts give them a sense of extreme confidence. They tend to have low self-esteem and are generally disappointed when they are not admired.

Borderline Personality Disorder

Requires five of the following symptoms:

1. Inappropriate behavior
2. Constant feelings of emptiness
3. Affective instability
4. Recurring suicide threats
5. Self-destructive impulsivity in at least two areas
6. Paranoid ideation/dissociative symptoms
7. Unstable self-image
8. Patterns of unstable and intense personal relationships (idealization and devaluation)
9. Fear of being abandoned

Histrionic Personality Disorder

Requires five of the following symptoms:

1. Physical appearance to draw attention
2. Believes relationships are intimate when they are not
3. Easily influenced by individuals
4. Exaggerated expression of emotion
5. Impressionistic speech
6. Shifting and shallow emotion
7. Inappropriate sexual provocation
8. Discomfort when not receiving attention needed

Narcissistic Personality Disorder

Requires five or more of the following symptoms:

1. Grandiose sense of self
2. Occupied with fantasies; includes level of power they have, success, brilliance
3. Feel they are unique
4. Require admiration
5. Sense of strong entitlement
6. Arrogant and conceited
7. Monopolize conversations and look down on others
8. Expect to be seen as superior and feel they can only be around other superior people
9. Take advantage of others

When these individuals feel criticized, they may react in the following manner:
*Angry and/or depressed when they don't receive the attention they feel they deserve
*Belittle others to make themselves feel superior

Chapter 6

Avoidant Personality Disorder
Schizotypal Disorder
Schizoid Disorder

Recommended theoretical orientation:

Cognitive Behavioral Therapy
Psychodynamic Therapy
Psychotherapy

Schizotypal	Schizoid	Avoidant Personality Disorder

All 3 Disorders = Social Deficits

Key Differences

AVOIDS social interaction due to fear of people.	FEELS NO DESIRE to form relationships, doesn't see the point, enjoys solitary lifestyle.	LACK of SOCIAL INTEREST & inadequacy due to fear of criticism.
Individuals with this disorder have difficulties forming and maintaining relationships. The individuals are characterized by pervasive social deficits, behavior oddities of cognition, inappropriate social cues, and misinterpretation of people's motivations.	Individuals are characterized by lack of interest in relationships with others, and limited emotional expression with others (coldness, detachment, or flattened affectivity).	Individuals are characterized by patterns of feeling inadequate, socially inhibited, and hypersensitivity. Feelings also involve anxiety or fearfulness.
Five of these symptoms must be present: • Excessive social anxiety • Ideas of reference • Odd beliefs/magical thinking • Lacks close friends (excluding family) • Bodily illusions • Suspiciousness/paranoid ideation • Inappropriate /constricted affect • Peculiarities in appearance or behavior	Four of these symptoms must be present: • Lacks close friends (excluding family) • Detachment or emotional coldness • Takes pleasure in few activities • Little interest in sexual relationships • Almost always chooses solitary activities • Indifferent to praise/criticism	Four of these symptoms must be present: • Fear of excelling in new situations – feels inadequate • Avoids activities that involve interpersonal contact • Sees self as unappealing, inferior, or socially incompetent • Reluctant to take risks or engage in threatening behavior • Preoccupied with being criticized or rejected • Fear of being shamed in an intimate relationships • Unwilling to interact with people who may not approve of them

Chapter 7

Brief Psychotic Disorder
Schizoaffective Disorder
Schizophrenia Disorder
Schizophreniform Disorder

Recommended theoretical orientation:

Cognitive Behavioral Therapy
Family Therapy
Psychotherapy
Medication

Schizoaffective	Schizophrenia
Key Differences	
The amount of time an individual experiences **severe mood** symptoms **accounts for more than half of the total duration of the illness.**	The individual may experience mood episodes, but the **duration of mood is brief** compared to the duration of the psychotic symptoms.
An individual who experiences persistent psychotic symptoms (schizophrenia symptoms) and major mood disorder (depression or bipolar disorder). Symptoms are present for at least two weeks and have to be present for most of the time and meet the criteria for a major mood disorder.	An individual who experiences psychosis (cannot tell the difference between real and imagined) is unable to express emotion or relate to others. Acute symptoms must be present for one month and continuous signs of symptoms present for at least six months. Symptoms are described as either positive or negative.
Two primary types are: • **Bipolar type** - requires at least one manic episode • **Depressive type** - requires only major depressive episodes	Must present two or more symptoms:
Symptoms include the following: • Delusions • Hallucinations • Disorganized speech • Grossly disorganized/ catatonic behavior • Negative symptoms **Bipolar type:** • Episodes of mania & sometimes major depression (see bipolar definition) **Depressive type:** • Depressed mood • Inability to sleep • Lack of energy • Feeling of guilt • Difficulty in concentration • Change in weight • Lack of pleasure in activities Schizoaffective symptoms overlap with bipolar, depressive disorder, and schizophrenia.	**Positive Symptoms:** • Delusions • Hallucinations • Grossly disorganized thinking and speech; catatonic behavior • Disorganized behavior - lack of proper hygiene, choosing the appropriate clothing for the weather, impulsive actions **Negative symptoms:** • Flat affect • Lack of pleasure in life • Inability to start/ continue productive activities • Limited ability to engage in conversation with others • Lack of motivation • Withdrawal from social activities, friends and family **Cognitive symptoms:** • Poor executive functioning • Poor working memory • Trouble focusing

Brief Psychotic Disorder	Schizophreniform

Key Differences

Symptoms of psychotic behavior are in response to trauma and last for less than a month.	Symptoms are similar to schizophrenia, but duration of symptoms sets the diagnosis for Schizophreniform.
The individual experiences psychotic symptoms due to extreme trauma, stress, assault, or death of a loved one.	The individual experiences psychosis (cannot tell the difference between real and imagined) for at least one month but less than six months. This disorder is on the schizophrenia spectrum and needs two major symptoms for diagnosis.
Symptoms are present for at least one day and less than one month.	Symptoms last for at least one month but less than six months. Must present two symptoms (one must be either 1, 2, or 3):
• Delusions • Hallucinations • Disorganized speech • Grossly disorganized/catatonic behavior	1. Delusions 2. Hallucinations 3. Disorganized speech 4. Abnormal body movements, repeating motions over and over 5. Negative symptoms

Chapter 8

Delusional Disorder
Depersonalization/Derealization Disorder
Dissociative Amnesia Disorder
Dissociative Identity Disorder
Paranoid Personality Disorder

Recommended theoretical orientation:

Cognitive Behavioral Therapy
Family Therapy
Psychotherapy

Delusional Disorder	Paranoid Personality Disorder

Individual has elaborate, non-bizarre delusion and expresses emotions **CONSISTENT WITH BELIEFS**

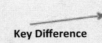

Key Difference

IRRATIONAL FEAR or PARANOIA that someone intends to harm them

The individual is characterized by either bizarre or non-bizarre presence of delusions for at least one month or longer. The individual does not meet the criteria for schizophrenia.

Aside from the delusions, the individual's functioning is not impaired, and behavior is not bizarre or odd enough to affect daily functioning.

The following are different types of delusions:

Erotomanic:
The individual believes that an important person (famous person) is in love with them.

Grandiose:
The individual has an over-inflated sense of self. Presence of persistent delusion.

Jealous type:
The individual continuously believes that his or her partner or spouse is unfaithful to the relationship.

Persecutory:
The individual believes they are being spied on and others are out to get them.

Somatic type:
The individual believes they have a medical issue or physical defects.

Mixed types:
The individual has two or more of the delusions listed above.

The individual displays a continuous pattern of suspicion of others and is difficult to get along with. The individual assumes that personal and professional relationships have malignant motives towards them.

Individual must have had at least four or more of the following symptoms:

1. Fear or anxiety is out of proportion to the actual threat
2. Doubts the trustworthiness of others
3. Hesitant to confide in others
4. Suspicions of a partner's fidelity without justification
5. Reads hidden meanings into remarks
6. Maintains constant grudges
7. Believes attacks on his/her character by others
8. Believes in conspiracy theories
9. Constantly feels threatened by loved ones and/or strangers

Dissociative Identity Disorder (formerly Multiple Personality Disorder)	Dissociative Amnesia	Depersonalization/ Derealization Disorder

Dissociative Disorders are frequently associated with previous trauma in an individual's life. Symptoms involve disturbances of mental functioning.

When two or more personalities (identity fragments) exist within a person's identity. Individuals with this disorder are often victims of severe abuse.	The inability to recall important personal information about self, not to be confused with normal forgetfulness.	When an individual feels detached from themselves; looking into self from the outside. Individual is aware of how they feel and see the world, but can't explain why this is happening.

Symptoms:

- The personalities are dominant at particular times/ situations. Each personality has its own sense of self
- The identity is a change in behavior and consciousness, cognition, and perception
- Memory loss includes not remembering people, places, events, or personal information
- Sense of detachment from self, causing distress or impairment in social occupation function and other areas of functioning

Variations include:

Localized
- The inability to recall an event or a period of time

Selective
- The inability to recall a specific event or period of time

Generalized
- The inability to recall one's own life history

Depersonalization
- The individual can feel detached, as if they are outside their bodies. The individual feels they are watching events from the outside - not being in the now.

Derealizaton
- The individual feels that things, events, and people aren't real

Chapter 9

Antisocial Personality Disorder
Conduct Disorder
Disruptive Mood Dysregulation Disorder
Intermittent Explosive Disorder
Oppositional Defiant Disorder

Recommended theoretical orientation:

Behavior Therapy
Cognitive Behavioral Therapy
Parent Child Interaction Therapy
Parent Training
Psychotherapy

Oppositional Defiant Disorder	Conduct Disorder	Antisocial Personality Disorder
Children (age 3-18)	Appears before age 10 - by age 16	Adult

Patterns of argumentative behavior and attitudes toward authority figures. **Key Characteristic: Fighting Against Being Controlled**	Serious emotional and behavioral problems in adolescents and children. **Key Characteristic: Will Attempt To Control Others**	**Emotional, erratic, and dramatic behaviors. A lack of concern toward the rights and feelings of others**
Symptoms must disrupt their school, social, and home life and be present for at least six months. **Children under 5: The behaviors occur on most days for at least six months. For** some children, symptoms may only show in one environment - home.	**Symptoms commonly begin by the age of 16.** At least three of these behaviors must have occurred within the past year with one occurring within the past six months.	The following criteria must be met: •**Must be at least 18** •**History of conduct disorder before age of 15** •**Has shown at least 3 of the following symptoms before the age of 15:**
Category I (often) •Easily loses temper •Frequently touchy or easily annoyed •Angry or resentful	**Category I** Aggressive behaviors toward people and animals, including bullying, intimidating people, physical violence, forced sexual acts, weapon use, or inflicting physical cruelty to people or animals.	•Irritability/aggression •Deceitfulness •Impulsivity •Reckless disregard for the safety of self and others •Lack of remorse
Category II (often) •Argues with adults and/or authority figures •Actively defies and/or refuses to comply with rules and requests from authority figures •Deliberately annoys others •Blames others for their mistakes or misbehavior	**Category II** Has deliberately engaged in property destruction or setting fires. **Category III** •Has broken into someone's home, building, or car and stolen something •Often lies to gain goods or favors or to avoid obligations	•Failure to conform to social norms and laws •Consistent irresponsibility
Category III •Often vindictive or spiteful •Has been spiteful or vindictive at least twice within the past six months	**Category IV** •Often stays out late at night, despite parental rules (before age of 13) •Has run away from home overnight at least twice without returning for a long period of time •Is often truant from school (before the age of 13)	

Intermittent Explosive Disorder	Disruptive Mood Dysregulation Disorder
(Late Childhood - Adolescence)	(Children - Teenagers)

This disorder involves repeated, sudden episodes of impulsive, aggressive, and/or angry verbal outbursts, in which the individual reacts disproportionately to the situation.

Symptoms occur suddenly, with no warning, and usually last less than 30 minutes.

Aggressive:
- Verbal aggression
- Rage
- Irritability
- Increased energy

The outbursts can include:
- Temper tantrums
- Elevated arguments
- Tirades
- Shouting
- Slapping or shoving
- Destruction or damage of property and/or physical assault involving physical injury against individuals or animals

This disorder involves persistent, irritable, or angry moods and frequent temper outbursts that are disproportionate to the situation. Similar to ODD and Bipolar. **Diagnosis is new, therefore effective therapy treatment is in new stages of effectiveness.**

Symptoms must be present before the age of 10 and not after the age of 18. Diagnosis is not to be made before the age of six.

Symptoms must be present for 12 months:
- Often irritable or angry for most of the day
- Frequent severe temper outbursts that are out of proportion to the situation occur an average of three times a week
- Temper is inconsistent
- The temper outbursts are present at home and in school

Chapter 10

Obsessive Compulsive Disorder
Obsessive Compulsive Personality Disorder

Recommended theoretical orientation:

Cognitive Behavior Therapy
Exposure and Response Prevention
Psychodynamic
Psychotherapy

Obsessive Compulsive Disorder	Obsessive Compulsive Personality Disorder

Key Difference

OCD is an ANXIETY disorder. Presence of true OBSESSION and/or COMPULSION.	OCPD is STRICT ADHERENCE to orderliness and control over one's environment at the expense of flexibility to new experiences.

Characterized by an individual's disturbing thoughts of obsessions or compulsions (some individuals may have both) that impact their daily lives. Some individuals may spend an hour a day on these behaviors.

Obsessions include:
- Continuous, persistent thoughts that cause distress. Attempts to ignore the thoughts, urges, images, and causes that lead to the compulsive behavior
- Unfounded suspicion of individuals
- Need for orderliness
- Need for cleanliness; fear of germs

Compulsions:
- Repetitive behaviors in which the individual feels inclined to perform in response to an obsession
- Repetitive behaviors include: washing of hands, performing certain tasks a certain number of times, checking appliances a certain number of times
- Behavioral acts are aimed at reducing anxiety or distress or preventing a feared event

Characterized by strict adherence to orderliness and control. The control over their environment makes the individual inflexible and not open to new experiences.

Symptoms include:
- Preoccupation with details, rules, and organization that affect the job at hand and make one inefficient
- Perfectionism that interferes with daily tasks at work, school, or home
- Excessive devotion to the productivity of a job, which jeopardizes social life
- Is overly diligent about values and morals
- Has a difficult time discarding old objects and materials that provide no use
- Tendency to have black and white thinking and stubbornness
- Hesitant to work with others
- When working with others, the need for control is prevalent
- Difficulty expressing emotions and feelings, affects relationships
- Has difficulty maintaining relationships

Obsessive Compulsive
Personality Disorder

Is
OBSESSED WITH

INEFFICIENT

- ➤ Schedules
- ➤ Details
- ➤ Rules
- ➤ Perfectionism
- ➤ Orderliness
- ➤ Complete Control

- ➤ Spends extra time with planning and worrying

ALSO inflexible, easily stressed, and tends to be rigid in beliefs and moral issues

Obsessive Compulsive Disorder	Obsessive Personality Disorder

EGO - DYSTONIC – wishes they could stop

Key Difference

EGO - SYNTONIC – happy with how they are, don't want to change

Obsessions	Compulsions	Obsessions	
Germs	Cleaning	Perfectionism	Inefficient
Feels unsafe	Checking	Control	• Spends too much time planning and/or worrying
Bad things will happen	Repeating	Rules	
	Arranging	Details	• Very rigid with moral issues and beliefs
Discord		Schedules	
		Orderliness	• Is perceived as stubborn

Chapter 11

Attention Deficit/Hyperactivity Disorder (ADHD)
Autism Spectrum Disorder (ASD)
Neurodevelopmental Disorders

Recommended theoretical orientation:

Cognitive Behavioral Therapy
Behavioral Therapy
Parent Training
Psychotherapy
Strengthening skills, multimodal teaching

Attention Deficit/Hyperactivity Disorder (ADHD)	Autism Spectrum Disorder (ASD)

Key Difference

Difficult to concentrate, pay attention, sit still, and/or limit impulsivity.	Neurodevelopmental condition that causes challenges with social skills, communication, and thinking – repetitive behavior is part of diagnosis.
May be eligible for IEP "Other Health Component" – Accommodations can be provided under a 504 plan.	May be eligible for IEP "Autism." Special Education may be provided with accommodations.

Must present at least six symptoms of inattention AND/OR hyperactivity-impulsivity.

Onset before the age of 12 and persists for at least six months.

Inattentive type
- Frequently loses items
- Forgetfulness
- Easily distracted by extraneous stimuli
- Fails to complete chores or schoolwork
- Difficulty sustaining participation in activities and tasks
- Difficulty listening when addressed
- Avoids tasks that require focus

Hyperactive-impulsive type
- Intrudes on others' space/time
- Difficulty playing quietly
- Running in inappropriate settings
- Fidgeting or squirming in a seat/looks to get out of seat
- Excessive talking
- Always seems restless
- Interrupts often

Two categories for diagnosis of autism spectrum disorder:

Impairment in social interactions and in communication:
- Poor eye contact
- Delayed speech or loss of speech
- Lack of ability to express emotions or feelings
- Inappropriate social interaction; disruptive, aggressive
- Lack of ability to sustain or initiate conversation
- Speaks with abnormal rhythm
- Lack of developmentally appropriate play
- Absence of developmentally appropriate relationships (peer)
- Lack of ability to recognize nonverbal cues, such as interpreting other people's facial expressions, body language

Behavior patterns may include:
- Performs repetitive movements, such as hand flapping
- Has difficulty with coordination, such as clumsiness or walking on toes
- Has fascination with detail of objects, but doesn't understand the function of the object, such as the wheel on a toy car
- Has high abnormal focus
- Has specific food preferences
- Has specific routines and/or rituals

Noticeable specific behavior patterns:
Lack of eye contact - disinterest in others – rarely reaches out to others – repeating the words of others – obsessive interest in narrow subjects – extreme emphasis on routine and consistency.

Communication Disorders	Learning Disorders	Motor Disorders
Disorders that affect the ability to apply language and speech with other individuals.	Interferes with an individual's ability to learn basic skills: reading, writing, and math.	Involves coordination disorders, stereotypic movement disorder, and tic disorder (formerly Tourette's Disorder).
Symptoms: Speech disorder – difficulty in making speech sounds. Fluency disorder (stuttering) – begins between the ages of two and seven. Speech is repetitive, has hesitations or disturbance in flow. Language disorder – has difficulty in relaying their meaning to others using speech.	Common disabilities include: •Dyslexia •ADHD •Dysgraphia •Dyscalculia •Processing defects **Symptoms:** Spelling incorrectly Difficulty with syntax and grammar Difficulty reading Difficulty with understanding what is read Difficulty with math calculation Difficulty with math reasoning	**Coordination Disorder** •Clumsiness •Delayed sitting, walking, and crawling •Difficulty with jumping, standing on one foot (gross motor skills) •Difficulty with writing, tying shoes (fine motor skills) **Stereotypic Movement Disorder (symptoms are repetitive and excessive)** •Head banging •Rocking back and forth •Hitting oneself •Biting oneself •Nail biting **Tourette's Disorder** •Simple tics involve brief/sudden repetitive movements – usually small movements •Complex tics involve larger complex movements •Vocal tics are random short words or sounds. **Persistent vocal or motor tic disorders include:** •Vocal sounds •Arm, leg or head jerking •Eye blinking •Unspecified tic •Other specified tic

Treatment for these disorders consists of:
•Psychoeducation
•Psychotherapy
•Cognitive therapy
•Strengthening skills, multimodal teaching

Chapter 12

Delirium
Alzheimer's Disease
Huntington's Disease
Parkinson's Disease

Neurocognitive Disorders: (previously known as Dementia)

Conditions that lead to an individual's cognitive decline. These declines affect attention, memory, learning, perception, language, and social cognition.

Recommended theoretical orientation:

Family Therapy
Group Therapy
Psychoeducation
Psychotherapy
Medication

Delirium	Alzheimer's Disease	Huntington's Disease	Parkinson's Disease
Significant deficit in cognition or memory compared to an individual's previous function.	A degenerative condition. No cure. Usually occurs after the age of 65.	A degenerative breakdown of cells in the brain. It is also an inherited disease. Appears between the ages of 30 and 40.	A progressive disorder of the nervous system that affects movement.
Risk groups: Elderly Burn victims Drug users	**Stage 1:** 1-3 years Mild amnesia Diminished visuospatial skill Indifference Irritability Sadness Anomia		
Symptoms: Inability to stay focused Inability to articulate Easily distracted Withdrawn from activities **Cognitive:** Poor memory Disorientation Difficulty recalling words or speaking	**Stage 2:** 2-10 years Increased amnesia Restlessness Flat mood Delusions Aphasia Acalculia Inability to translate ideas (actions/movement)	Symptoms vary amongst individuals. One individual may experience more movement disorder, versus another other who may experience more cognitive disorders.	Symptoms develop differently in people.
Rambling speech Difficulty understanding speech Difficulty with reading or writing	**Stage 3:** 8-12 years Severely impaired functioning Apathy Limb rigidity Fecal and urinary incontinence	Irritability Depression Forgetfulness Dementia Fidgeting Clumsiness Involuntary quick jerks	Slow movement Resting tremors Loss of balance and/or coordination Violent restlessness Depression Dementia

Chapter 13

Avoidant/Restrictive Food Intake Disorder
Anorexia Nervosa
Bulimia Nervosa
PICA

Recommended theoretical orientation:

Cognitive Behavioral Therapy
Family Therapy
Psychotherapy

Anorexia Nervosa	Bulimia Nervosa

Key difference

Significantly Low Body Weight	Normal Body Weight
• Extreme restriction of food • Irrational fear of gaining weight • Irrational behaviors that prevent weight gain • Distorted body image Lose weight by fasting, excessive exercise, and dieting. Binge/purging types eat excessive amount of food and then vomit.	A persistent concern with body weight and shape. At least one episode per week for three months. • Consuming amounts of food that are larger than most individuals would eat within the same time period • The individual feels a lack of control over eating Binge eating followed by purging. Self-induced vomiting, laxatives, fasting; extreme exercise in order to prevent weight gain.

PICA	Avoidant/Restrictive Food Intake
Persistent eating of non-food substances. Most common in children and pregnant women. Symptoms must be present for at least one month. Children will also eat regular food. • Paint • Pebbles • Hair • Sand	The individual consumes only certain foods (also know as "picky eating"). The choice of food is based on texture, appearance, smell, taste, and prior previously bad experiences with certain foods. This often results in nutrition deficiencies. **Symptoms:** • Inadequate food intake (results in nutritional deficiencies) • Adults - weight loss. In children - failure to gain weight • Psychosocial decline • Supplements are used to maintain needed nutrients • Individual does not have distorted body image or medical condition

Chapter 14

Nicotine
Alcohol Intoxication & Withdrawal
Amphetamine and Cocaine Intoxication & Withdrawal

Treatment for Substance Abuse Disorder consists of:
Family Therapy
Medication
Psychoeducation
Psychotherapy
Specific Support Group (Narconon, AA)

Nicotine Addiction and Withdrawal	Alcohol Intoxication and Withdrawal	Amphetamine and Cocaine Intoxication and Withdrawal
Individual is dependent on nicotine. The effects of nicotine include: enhanced memory, improved concentration, appetite suppression, respiration increase, and hypertension. **Withdrawal symptoms:** • Inability to concentrate • Inability to focus • Anxiety • Weight gain • Agitation • Depression	**Symptoms of intoxication:** • Slurred speech • Poor coordination • Uncontrolled eye movements • Impairment of memory and/or attention • Psychological changes/ maladaptive behavior (sexual/aggressive behavior, impaired judgment) • Coma • Gait is affected **Withdrawal symptoms:** • Hand tremors • Insomnia • Vomiting and/or nausea • Anxiety • Agitation, psychomotor • Long use can cause seizures • Hallucinations/illusions **Withdrawal delirium:** • Hallucinations • Delusions • Agitation • Cognitive disturbances	Amphetamine and cocaine are two different drugs that vary in effect. Cocaine (**illegal**) stimulates the central nervous system, causing a feeling of euphoria. Amphetamine also induces euphoria, but is a **legal** drug used for those with ADHD, narcolepsy, and severe cases of fatigue. **Symptoms of intoxication:** • Seizures • Confusion • Muscle weakness • Nausea and/or vomiting • Weight loss • Agitation • Dilated pupils • Hypertension • Psychological changes/ maladaptive behavior (sexual/ aggressive behavior, impaired judgment, paranoid ideation, auditory hallucinations, euphoria, anger) **Withdrawal symptoms:** • Fatigue • Unpleasant dreams • Insomnia and/or hypersomnia • Increase in appetite • Severe depression • Retardation and/or psychomotor agitation

Chapter 15

Sleep/Wake Disorders

Recommended theoretical orientation:

Cognitive Behavior Therapy
Behavioral Therapy
Medication

Insomnia	Circadian Rhythm Sleep-Wake	Non-Rapid Eye Movement Arousal	Rapid Eye Movement Disorder
When an individual has difficulty falling asleep and/or staying asleep. Starts in young adulthood. • Must occur at least three nights a week • Must occur for at least three months • Must cause significant distress in functioning **Variations:** **Episodic** - lasts under three months **Persistent** - lasts longer than three months **Recurrent** - several episodes in a year	An individual's inability to go to sleep and wake up on time for social needs, work, and school. **Symptoms:** • Individual fails to fall asleep until late at night and results in oversleeping	Individual's brain is partially awake and partly in REM sleep. Experiences • Sleep walking • Sleep terrors • Sleep sex During sleep time, the individual can perform actions without being aware.	An individual will awaken from REM sleep and act out their dreams: shouting, hitting, punching, and getting out of bed.

Breathing-Related	Hypersomnolence	Narcolepsy	Nightmare Disorder
When an individual's breathing is interrupted during sleep snoring. There are three types: **Obstructive Sleep Apnea** • The individual's upper airway closes, partly or fully, but breathing continues **Central Sleep Apnea** • The individual's respiration ceases because of a decrease in ventilatory drive **Mixed Sleep Apnea** • The individual shows signs of both OSA and CSA	Excessive sleep in the daytime or at night. Individual often naps during the day. **Symptoms -** occurs at least three times a week for at least one month (acute condition) or three months (persistent) • Causes distress in function (social, occupational) • Not associated due to another disorder, medical reason, medication, or drugs	Individual experiences sleep during the day and attacks of sudden sleep during the day. **Symptoms:** • Hallucinations • Excessive daytime sleep • Loss of muscle tone and muscle control • Inability to move or speak	An individual experiences nightmares, which often cause distress. The disturbing nightmares prevent an individual from getting enough sleep.

Chapter 16

Factitious Disorder
Conversion Disorder
Illness Disorder
Malingering
Somatic Symptom Disorder

Recommended theoretical orientation:

Cognitive Behavior Therapy
Psychotherapy

Factitious Disorder	An individual intentionally manifests physical or psychological symptoms in order to satisfy the need to fill the role of a sick person: 1. Presents an illness in an exaggerated manner 2. Avoids questioning from others that may expose the truth 3. May undergo multiple surgeries 4. May undergo medical procedures 5. May hide insurance claim forms from others 6. Voluntary
Malingering Disorder	Physical symptoms to avoid a specific activity, such as going to work or receiving an award: 1. Individual obtains medical evaluation for legal reasons and may also apply for insurance compensation 2. Individual has a marked inconsistency between the complaint and the findings. Individual does not cooperate with diagnostic evaluation or treatment 3. Individual has an antisocial personality disorder 4. Voluntary
Somatic Symptom Disorder	Individual may suggest a medical condition exists but isn't explainable: 1. Symptoms are dramatic and overstated 2. Worries extensively about the symptoms. Spends a lot of time worrying about health issues 3. Worrying causes distress 4. Recurrent complaints (a symptom may be present for six months) 5. No medical explanation has been found
Conversion Disorder	The loss of bodily function or serious physical disease: 1. Individual may become blind, mute, or paralyzed due to an acute stressor 2. Vomiting, coughing spells, or hyperesthesia may develop 3. The symptoms tested do not reveal underlying disease 4. Sensory loss, movement loss, or repetition of movements that are not intentional 5. May be used to maintain internal conflict 6. May be used by a person to avoid an activity 7. Not voluntary
Illness Anxiety Disorder	A preoccupation with having; getting a serious illness (formally hypochondriasis). Symptoms must be present for six months: 1. Anxiety is disproportionate to the symptoms 2. Great knowledge about their condition will go to several doctors to confirm their illness 3. Frequent doctor visits 4. May avoid health facilities for fear of being diagnosed with an illness 5. May avoid places and people for fear of getting sick

Chapter 17

Sexual Dysfunctions

Transvestic

Frotteuristic

Exhibitionistic

Voyeuristic

Fetishistic

Gender Dysphoria

Recommended theoretical orientation:

Behavior Therapy
Cognitive Therapy
Group Therapy
Psychodynamic
Psychoeducation
Psychotherapy

Delayed/Premature Ejaculation	Erectile Disorder	Male Hypoactive Sexual Desire Disorder
Delayed - Also known as impaired ejaculation. Symptoms must be present for at least three months: •Prolonged period of sexual stimulation for a man to ejaculate •Can occur in all sexual situations or with certain partners (situational delayed ejaculation) •Symptoms cause stress for the individual •Condition is not caused by another medical condition **Premature – when ejaculation occurs sooner than a man and partner would like during sex.** **Symptoms:** •Conditions are present for at least six months •Ejaculation occurs in under a minute •Condition causes frustration, stress, and tension between partners •Symptoms cause stress for the individual •Condition must not be caused by a medical condition	The inability for a man to get and or keep an erection firm enough for sex. Symptoms are present for at least six months. One or more symptoms must be present. **Symptoms:** •Unable to get an erection •Unable to maintain an erection during sex Symptoms can be situational or occur all the time.	A lack of sexual fantasies and/or desire for sexual activity. Symptoms present for at least six months: •Low sexual desire over 50% of the time •Delay or absence of orgasm during sex •Ejaculates within under a minute •Causes stress to the individual

Female Orgasmic Disorder	Female Sexual Interest/Arousal Disorder	Female Genito-Pelvic Pain Disorder
When an individual has difficulty reaching orgasm. Symptoms must be present for six months and not be explained by a medical condition:	The inability or persistent ability for a women to either achieve or maintain sexual arousal.	The difficulty of having sex because of significant pain during intercourse.
•Includes unsatisfying orgasm •Taking long to climax •Can occur during sex or masturbation •Causes distress	Three or more symptoms must be present for at least six months: •Lack of interest in sexual activity •Absence of thoughts of sexual activity •Lack of initiating sexual encounters •Lack of pleasure during sex •Causes distress for women •Not caused by a medical condition	Symptoms must be present for six months. One or more symptoms must be present: •Pain in the genital/pelvic area during sex causes tightening •Fear of sex because of the anticipated pain •Tightening of the pelvis when attempting intercourse •Avoiding sex

Transvestic	These fantasies or behaviors must be present for at least six months and cause severe distress (dysfunction in social settings or other areas of daily life). Recurrent and intense sexual arousal from cross dressing.
Frotteuristic	These acts are more often seen in males between the ages of 15 and 25. These acts continue for more than six months. The disorder involves intense fantasies, sexual arousal, urges that are centered on the act of touching/rubbing on non-consenting people. These behaviors are repetitive and usually occur in crowded places.
Exhibitionistic	The individual has recurrent urges over a period of six months. This disorder is marked by an individual's urge or fantasy of exposing one's genitals to unsuspecting people.
Voyeuristic	The individual must experience the disorder for at least six months and must be at least 18 years old. This disorder is marked by an individual's arousal from a fantasy or act of watching unsuspecting people who are naked, or partially clothed. The individual is not interested in having sex with the individuals being observed.
Fetishistic	The individual must experience the fetish arousal for at least six months. The fantasies cause significant distress or affect occupation and personal functioning. This disorder is characterized as an intense sexual arousal from the use of an inanimate object that causes distress or impairment. This disorder interferes with normal sexual functioning and arousal is impossible without the fetish object (high heels or other shoes, leather clothing, undergarments, toes, hair, feet). Sexual gratification can only be obtained with the fetish.

Gender Dysphoria

Appears in children (2 yrs) through adulthood

The individual strongly identifies with the opposite gender.

Symptoms in Children – must be present for six months:
•Incongruence with their own gender
•Strong desire to be the other gender
•Crossdressing (boys)
•Wears masculine clothing (girls)
•During play the child will have preference to role play the opposite gender
•During play the child chooses toys intended for the opposite gender
•Uncomfortable with their own anatomy
•Children are distressed in areas of relationships

Symptoms in Adolescents and Adults:
•Incongruence with their expressed gender, sexual organs, and characteristics (the incongruence is present for at least six months)
•The desire to have the sex characteristics of the other gender
•The desire to be the other gender, includes wanting to be treated like the other gender and wanting to think like the other gender.
•Excessive stress in relationships, family, friends, and social settings

Theoretical Orientation: Psychotherapy

This therapy will help the individual:
•Talk over fears they have
•Learn coping skills
•Learn to process and deal with the distress of feelings
•Discuss family alienation/support/acceptance
•Discuss society's acceptance and alienation

Chapter 18

Paraphilic Disorders: Paraphilia

Sexual Masochism Disorder
Sexual Sadism Disorder

Recommended theoretical orientation:

Cognitive Behavioral Therapy
Medication

Sexual Masochism Disorder	Sexual Sadism Disorder
Recurrent sexual fantasies, urges, and behavior that cause severe harm to self and/or others. Symptoms are present for at least six months and must be real acts, not fantasies. Sexual acts include asphyxiophilia, suffering, or humiliation. • Causes distress in areas of functioning - social/occupational • Beaten • Bound • Other ways an individual can suffer	Constant fantasies in which sexual excitement results from inflicting physical or psychological suffering on a partner. These acts are seen as power over the victim. Will never seek treatment on their own. Can include: • Humiliation • Terror • Rape • Torture • Murder

Pedophilic Disorder
Intense sexual arousal with fantasies or behaviors involving prepubescent adolescents (usually under the age of 13). Urges are present for six months. **Symptoms:** • Intense sexual fantasies • Urges or behaviors involving sexual activity with a prepubescent • Sexual urges have been acted on • The individual is at least 16 years old and 5 years older than the prepubescent

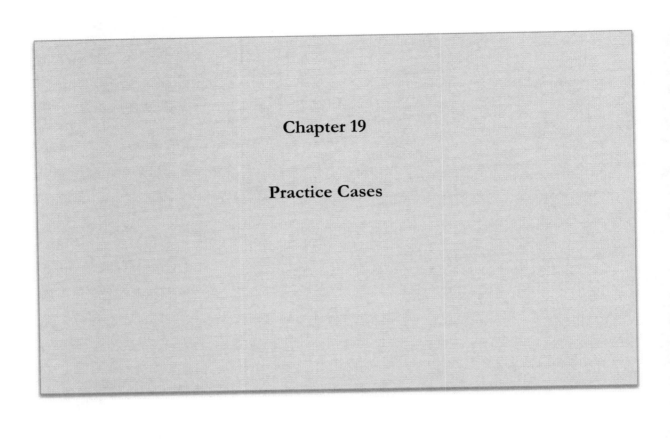

Chapter 19

Practice Cases

Tips

Carefully read the case.

Carefully read the questions given to you.

Does the answer apply to the question? Why?

Make your columns: dissect the question and answers.

Remember: Break the case down.

Presenting Problem	Symptoms	Duration	Diagnosis

The next several pages contain short cases to test your knowledge. This set-up will assist you with what to look for in your answers, the importance of the answer, how it applies to the question, and what is needed to formulate a diagnosis

Jacob is a 49-year-old man who comes to see you after his girlfriend of four years left him, seven weeks ago. His previous relationship lasted for two years. He's unable to sleep through the night, feels sad, and has occasional body aches – symptoms that lasted four months after the first break-up. He relates that lately his job has been stressful, and he's finding it difficult to concentrate. Once a social person, he now feels withdrawn. He shares that he hurt his ankle two weeks ago and is unable to exercise, adding to his misery and making him anxious. He says he has no thoughts of suicide and wants to feel better.

What is Jacob's presenting problem?

What are the presenting symptoms?

What is the duration?

What is Jacob's behavior?

What is Jacob's diagnosis?

Bonus: What theoretical orientation would you use?

It was a bright sunny day. Jenna was taking her usual walk, when she witnessed a man fall into a utility hole. While running over to see if she could help, she yelled to see if he was okay. He responded that he was, but had hurt his wrist. Ever since then, Jenna has experienced numbness, shortness of breath, trembling, and at times, some dizziness. Jenna now tries to avoid utility holes, as she fears someone falling in again. After six days, she finds herself feeling anxious and decides to see a therapist for help.

What is Jenna's presenting problem?

What are the presenting symptoms?

What is the duration?

What is Jenna's behavior?

What is Jenna's diagnosis?

Janet is a 19-year-old full-time college student, who works part-time at the school's health bar. She would like to join a few clubs at school, but is hesitant because her boyfriend doesn't seem interested in any of the school clubs. Billy is a 20-year-old full-time student who works part-time at the school bookstore. Janet states that their relationship was good, but that, lately, she is feeling depressed, alone, and not happy with Billy.

Billy loves doing things with Janet - they spend all their time together, and Billy relies on Janet's opinion and approval for everything. Janet hasn't been going out with friends or participating in any of the activities she enjoys because Billy doesn't feel comfortable. Janet knows Billy loves her, but she wants him to have a life separate from hers. Janet comes to you for help. She wants to see how you can help Billy, who is open to therapy.

Who is the identified client?

What is the presenting problem?

What is the duration?

What are the presenting symptoms?

What is Billy's diagnosis?

Anthony is a 40-year-old accountant who lives next door to his parents, with whom he has a close relationship. Anthony's father suffers from depression, but his mother has no history of mental health issues. Anthony comes to therapy because of his impulsive and excessive behavior, such as spending large sums of money on things he doesn't need, taking expensive vacations he can't afford, and buying new cars. His mother is concerned; she observes that this behavior occurs for a week, but that the effects create an abundance of stress and financial difficulties.

Anthony tells you that he sometimes feels depressed, and that his self-esteem and energy levels are deficient. At other times, however, he thinks that he's on a roll, does his best, and that no one is as good as him at his job. He doesn't understand what is going on and wants help from a therapist.

What is Anthony's presenting problem?

What are the presenting symptoms?

What is the duration?

What is Anthony's behavior?

What is Anthony's diagnosis?

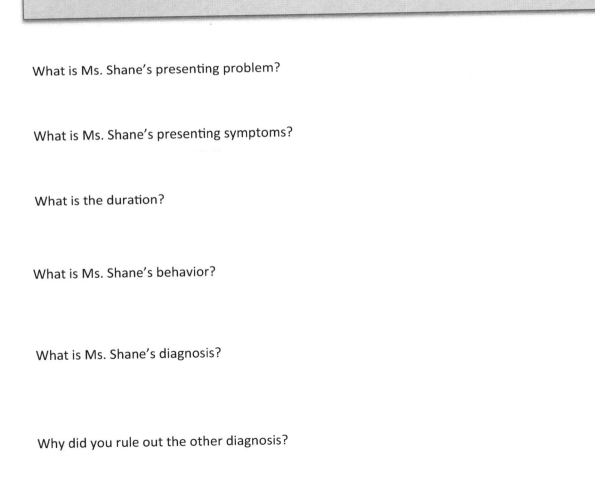

Ms. Shane has been referred to you by her doctor for evaluation. She is a 59-year-old woman in good physical health, but her doctor is concerned about her mental health. Ms. Shane is divorced, unemployed, and relies on family and friends to help her with daily tasks. She used to spend time with friends, going on short trips and to the movies, and volunteered on several committees in her community. Ms. Shane stopped participating in events and activities three weeks ago, and has not been herself. She tells you that she has always struggled to make herself have fun, but this time it has become a challenge.

Additionally, she tells you that she's having trouble following instructions, can't retain information, is forgetful and worried about unfulfilled tasks, and feels her family is not supportive. She is also having trouble sleeping, has loss of appetite, and feels her life isn't fulfilling. She has been having thoughts of death and has come to therapy for help.

What is Ms. Shane's presenting problem?

What is Ms. Shane's presenting symptoms?

What is the duration?

What is Ms. Shane's behavior?

What is Ms. Shane's diagnosis?

Why did you rule out the other diagnosis?

Lucy, a 23-year-old white female, was admitted to the hospital with auditory hallucinations, paranoia, and grandiose claims. She has no history of substance abuse, but has been noted for being withdrawn from interacting with people since the age of 16, after her mother died. She admitted herself to the hospital because she is fearful of her symptoms and wants help. She reports that she hears voices that say, "I am jealous of you." She wasn't able to determine the person's voice but feels it was someone who wants her money. She's worried that her condition will become public. Lucy says she is a very famous, wealthy person who meets other famous people all the time. You asked Lucy to elaborate regarding these people, but she was unable to provide details, telling you it was secret information. She states that she is in good health and full of energy. Her thoughts seem to be racing as she speaks. She confides in you that men are chasing after her, to be with her, because she's so special. You ask Lucy if she'd like to take some medication to calm down, but she becomes indignant and accuses you of being like the others who don't believe her because you're jealous.

What is Lucy's presenting problem?

What are the presenting symptoms?

What is the duration?

What is Lucy's behavior?

What is Lucy's diagnosis?

Edmond is a 39-year-old male. He is short and overweight, which makes him feel awkward. He also wears very tight fitting clothes, which are too small for him. He works as a cashier for the subway system. Edmond doesn't have many close friends. Edmond tries to meet friends through social apps (meetups). Lately, he has been feeling anxious, thinking that people are complicated.

Edmond comes to you because he is having problems maintaining friendships. He feels suspicious and says that people only want to talk to him because he's smart. He tells you about the social app he uses and that once he commits to attending these meetups, he experiences anxiety. Edmond starts to worry about what people are going to think about him. Edmond also feels that part of the reason he can't make friends is because he is so handsome, and people are jealous. You meet with Edmond, and notice that during the session he misses social cues. You also notice that his hair is not combed, and he makes noises when he's not speaking.

What is Edmond's presenting problem?

What are the presenting symptoms?

What is Edmond's behavior?

What is the duration?

What is Edmond's diagnosis?

Bonus: Why did you rule out the other diagnosis?

Tara is a four-year-old girl and an only child. Her parents both work full-time; she spends her days with her grandparents. Tara is an early riser, and is very loud when she wakes up, ignoring her parents' requests to be quieter (sometimes making even more noise). The last time Tara didn't follow the rules, she was punished. She is rarely happy with meals, and each one is a battle. She always wants something other than what's on the table. When Tara is given what she wants, she changes her mind. Her grandparents struggle, because she won't entertain herself. She demands that they play with her, and when they don't, she throws tantrums. Tara's grandparents have tried talking to her, but she gets angry with them, breaks toys, and throws things at them when she doesn't get her way. Tara tells her parents varied stories about why she's in trouble with her grandparents. She doesn't act this aggressively at home. Her parents go to therapy and tell you this behavior has been going on for the last 8 months. In addition to these concerns, she tells family members that she hates them and accuses them of not telling the truth.

What is Tara's presenting problem?

What are the presenting symptoms?

What is the duration?

What is Tara's behavior?

What is Tara's diagnosis?

Thomas is a seven-year-old boy. He is angry almost every day, and his continuous outbursts have gotten him into trouble at school. His mother meets with you and tells you that Thomas has tantrums at least three times a week, and is irritable most days of the week. He is also having problems with his friends – kids don't want to be around him. His mother tells you she's been dealing with this for over a year, and no longer knows how to handle the situation.

What is Thomas's presenting problem?

What are the presenting symptoms?

What is the duration?

What is Thomas's behavior?

What is Thomas's diagnosis?

Marcus is a six-year-old boy who is coming into therapy at the request of his mother, Gail. When Marcus and Gail meet with you, you notice that Marcus won't sit still. He is rude to his mother by interrupting her, and won't sit down. Marcus's mother asks him to sit down and behave, and he shouts back at her, "No." Gail tells you that she can't handle Marcus and needs help. She informs you that Marcus's aggressive and destructive behavior has been going on over the last three years. Marcus has been suspended from school, has broken items at home, abuses the family cat, and hits his sister.

What is Marcus's presenting problem?

What are the presenting symptoms?

What is the duration?

What is Marcus's behavior?

What is Marcus's diagnosis?

Cheryl is the owner of a gift shop in her local town. She works an eight-hour day, and currently employs four people. Cheryl's gift shop does very well, but this puzzles her because her employee turn-around is very high. Over the last two years, four people have quit, and she's fired five. Cheryl is frustrated because she can't find reliable employees. Procedures are in place to allow the gift shop to run smoothly. Every detail is written down, and she is proud to be entirely responsible for developing her system. Cheryl wants employees who will follow her procedures. A friend recommended that she try therapy. She readily agreed, because her stress level is high and she believes you can help.

What is Cheryl's presenting problem?

What are the presenting symptoms?

What is the duration?

What is Cheryl's behavior?

What is Cheryl's diagnosis?

Margo is a 19-year-old full-time college student. She is very competitive and has always excelled in both school and clubs. She comes from a family of doctors and lawyers, and the family standards are set high. Lately, Margo has been unable to sleep because she isn't doing well in one of her courses. Her roommate, Peggy, is concerned about Margo's palpable stress and has contacted you for help. Peggy tells you that Margo has neither been eating nor sleeping, weighs 95 pounds, and talks to herself. Peggy has informed Margo about the call, and she has agreed to see you. Peggy also tells you that Margo has lost 10 pounds this semester, and that Margo herself thinks she looks great. Margo shows up for her appointment looking frail and asks for help.

What is Margo's presenting problem?

What are the presenting symptoms?

What is the duration?

What is Margo's behavior?

What is Margo's diagnosis?

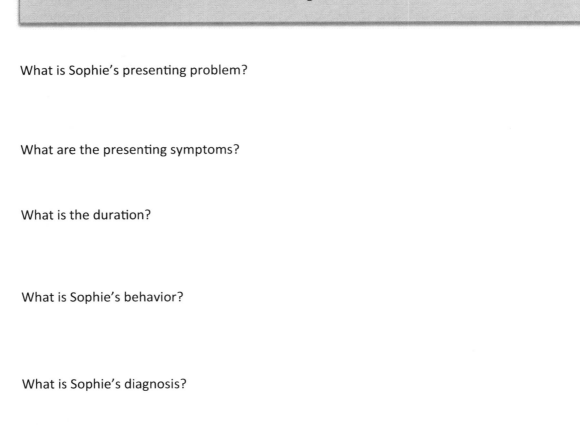

Sophie is a tall, slender, popular 15-year-old high school student, who maintains her weight at 98 pounds. She's a picky eater to stay fit for sports.

She has been experiencing crying episodes, sporadically, for several months. During these episodes, she tells her mother that she has stomachaches, headaches, feels tired and, at times, can't concentrate. Additionally, she hasn't been sleeping well and finds herself getting up every morning at 5:30 to prepare for the day.

Sophie does well in school, but often worries about her grades. She has many friends and is well-liked. Lately, however, she has been feeling out of place with her friends, and this worries her. Being part of the popular group is important to her, and if her friends were to drop her from the group, she'd be devastated. She is part of the swim team and captain of her cheerleading squad. Sophie tells you that she's been stressed for seven months and doesn't know how to control what she's feeling.

What is Sophie's presenting problem?

What are the presenting symptoms?

What is the duration?

What is Sophie's behavior?

What is Sophie's diagnosis?

Max is a 14-year-old boy, whose parents bring him to therapy because they don't know how to handle his behavior. They feel they've done everything they can, and now need help. Max is defiant and argumentative. He frequently skips school and sneaks out of the house at night while his parents are sleeping. He picks on his sisters and always hides their favorite toys when he thinks they're annoying him. He also argues about having to clean up his room and help with chores.

Max has missed several classes, doesn't complete homework assignments, is distracting in class, and disrespects school staff. The teachers are cautious when speaking to him, for fear of his outbursts. When he doesn't get his way, he is vindictive and aggressive, such as throwing books. His parents indicate that he doesn't do drugs, sleeps well, and eats regularly. Max perceives that his parents treat him like a baby and expect too much from him. He feels he should be able to do what he wants without his parents trying to control him.

What is Max's presenting problem?

What are the presenting symptoms?

What is the duration?

What is Max's behavior?

What is Max's diagnosis?

James is a 53-year-old man who comes to you for therapy. He says he's been feeling down lately and is having trouble falling asleep. His wife left him ten years ago, and his dog died seven months ago. He has an active social life and works a full-time job as the manager of an upscale bar; he gets along well with his co-workers. James, at times, feels out of it and doesn't know how to clear the fog – this concerns him. He has experienced this sadness for as long as he can remember, and has never been able to shake the sad feelings. When he's down, he withdraws from people and can't motivate himself to do the activities he usually enjoys.

What is James's presenting problem?

What are the presenting symptoms?

What is the duration?

What is James's behavior?

What is James's diagnosis?

Sal is a 24-year-old man. He was a mechanic in the army for six years, whose job was to assure the safety and reliability of Army vehicles. He was last stationed in the Middle East, and decided not to go back to the Army after he returned from tour. Sal has been home for twelve months, and lives with his parents. He has been dating Sara for the last eight months. Sal works as a mechanic at a nearby shop in his hometown. He works long days at the shop, because for the last nine months he has been going to work late. Sal has been unable to sleep, is easily startled, and is having a hard time remembering things. He's also having nightmares. Sara is worried about Sal, and calls you for help.

What is Sal's presenting problem?

What are the presenting symptoms?

What is the duration?

What is Sal's behavior?

What is Sal's diagnosis?

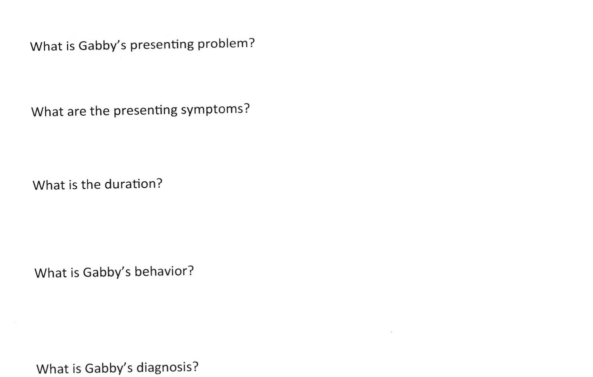

Gabby is a 44-year-old, divorced, unemployed woman who lives in a cottage on her parents' property. Gabby has a nurse, Joan, who cares for her on a daily basis. Joan has expressed concerns to Gabby's parents about Gabby's recent behavior. Joan states that for the last six weeks Gabby has been impulsive, talks to herself, is verbally abusive, and sleeps late in the morning. Joan is concerned about Gabby's behavior, and is starting to feel afraid Gabby may hurt her.

Joan talks Gabby into attending therapy. Gabby attends therapy and appears annoyed. She is very short with her comments. Gabby's appearance is disheveled – she wears wrinkled clothes, and her hair isn't combed. Gabby is angry that Joan is complaining about her behavior, and says her parents don't need to know her business. Gabby is blaming everyone else in her life for her problems. Gabby admits that lately she has been unable to sleep because she's been feeling paranoid. Gabby also states that her judgment has been impaired, and she feels muscle weakness. Gabby admits to you that she was a drug user four years ago.

What is Gabby's presenting problem?

What are the presenting symptoms?

What is the duration?

What is Gabby's behavior?

What is Gabby's diagnosis?

Doug and his wife, Gail, have been married for three months. Doug is a self-employed real estate broker, and Gail is a Director at a Community College. They make a good living, mostly due to Gail's job. Lately, Gail is starting to worry about Doug's behavior. Doug is highly competitive in the sales industry, and Gail has recently heard him complain that he's not able to sell because he can't tolerate stupid people. Doug has expressed that he is superior and highly intelligent, and because of this, potential homebuyers are scared off. Doug also says that he can't trust people, because they steal his ideas and are out to get him. Doug looks for ways to sell homes by trying to deceive the buyer. He doesn't care what it takes to get the sale, and knows his charm will close the deal. Doug feels he deserves the best.

Gail has also noticed that Doug doesn't have many friends. He can be brutally honest, and this has hurt many family members. Gail has tried talking to him, but he gets angry when he feels he's being criticized. Gail tells you that their sex life has dwindled to once a month, because Doug has told her she's not pretty enough and he could do better. Gail is uncertain about what's going on with Doug; she thinks maybe it is a phase. Gail talks Doug into attending therapy. Doug tries to belittle you during the session.

What is Doug's presenting problem?

What are the presenting symptoms?

What is the duration?

What is Doug's behavior?

What is Doug's diagnosis?

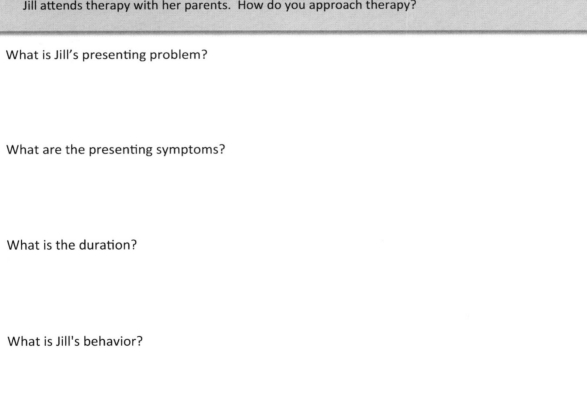

Jill is a 12-year-old student. She has two brothers, ages 16 and 19. Jill has been struggling with concerns about herself. She has felt, since the age of 6 years old, like she's a boy in a girl's body. Jill has shared this with her brothers and they have always brushed it off. They tell her that it's in her head, and that she feels like that because she doesn't have a sister.

When Jill was younger, she always played with her brothers' toys and wanted to dress like them. Jill never had a desire to dress up like a girl, and hates the "girlie" clothes her mother buys her. Jill has always felt uncomfortable about her body and now she is stressed about the way her body is developing. Jill has been wearing baggy clothes to cover herself up.

Jill meets with her guidance counselor because her grades are poor and she's having problems with her friends. Her teachers have noticed Jill has isolated herself from the other kids. Jill tells her guidance counselor that she's unhappy because she's a boy in a girl's body. Jill also tells her counselor that she's tried to tell her parents but they just feel it's because she has two brothers and these feelings will pass. Jill wants to see a therapist. How do you approach Jill's parents?

Jill attends therapy with her parents. How do you approach therapy?

What is Jill's presenting problem?

What are the presenting symptoms?

What is the duration?

What is Jill's behavior?

What is Jill's diagnosis?

Liza is a 41-year-old waitress who works in a very hip bar in the city. Liza has a ten-year-old daughter and seven-year-old son. Liza's husband, Steve, left her eight years ago. Steve finally left Liza because he could not handle her neediness and privative ways.

Liza needs constant attention and dresses very provocatively. Her employer has to regularly remind her to dress a little more conservatively, as her co-workers are bothered by the way she dresses. Liza looks for attention, and when she doesn't get the attention she needs, she can become very moody. Liza is always looking to pick up the "right" customer. She wants a man who will cherish her. Liza has dated many customers from the bar, and many stay away from her because they know she makes up stories about how in love a man is with her. Liza is also manipulative and shallow, and has a tendency to exaggerate. Her employer has become concerned with her and recommends that she seek therapy. Liza thinks he's crazy, but is willing to go because she needs this job.

What is Liza's presenting problem?

What are the presenting symptoms?

What is the duration?

What is Liza's behavior?

What is Liza's diagnosis?

Don is a 34-year-old man who lives with his grandmother. Don's parents passed away when he was 12, and because of his good relationship with his grandmother, he chose to live with her. Don adjusted well to his new living arrangements.

Don did exceptionally well in school, and made honor roll every quarter during high school. He struggled with relationships, as people felt he was arrogant and cold, and lacked regard for people's feelings. Because of his treatment towards others, he was not liked by many students or teachers.

Don felt he knew everything, and mocked others because they weren't as smart as him. He didn't attend many school functions or participate in clubs because he felt people were stealing his ideas and he couldn't trust anyone. Don dated Joyce when he was a junior in high school. Joyce was Don's first girlfriend, and the relationship lasted for two months. Joyce could not tolerate his lack of trust, his grudges, and his accusations against her. Don continued on to college, graduated, and met Chloe, who he ended up marrying. In the last five years, Don has had three jobs, Chloe left him, and he is presently unemployed. Don was let go from his employment because he accused others of wanting to steal ideas from him, held grudges with co-workers, misconstrued most of his employer's requests, and accused co-workers of constantly attacking his character. Chloe left Don because she couldn't take the continuous lack of trust and constant jealousy. His grandmother calls you because she doesn't know how to help Don.

What is Don's presenting problem?

What are the presenting symptoms?

What is the duration?

What is Don's behavior?

What is Don's diagnosis?

Phil is a 46-year-old man who is presently serving a six-year prison term for defrauding people. Phil set up a scam and stole thousands of dollars over several years from innocent people. His victims lost their life savings. Phil is up for review, and part of the review process is the requirement to attend therapy. You meet with Phil to determine if he is ready for early release.

Phil enters the room, and you can tell he doesn't want to attend. He covers it up with a fake smile and asks you how you're doing. You, in return, ask him the same, and he replies, "Fabulous." You then ask him how he feels about the required counseling session. Phil states he's a changed man and looking forward to getting on with his life. Phil looks away as he says this to you, and as he glances away, you notice a smirk. You ask Phil how he feels about the crime he committed. Phil responds by saying that people make their own choices, and they chose to invest with him and that was their problem. He states that those people had plenty of money that they didn't need, and he needed money to survive. As Phil continues to talk, he becomes aggressive and clearly shows a lack of remorse for his role. Phil feels that people need to learn how to protect themselves, and it's not his problem if they don't know how. You ask Phil about his personal life. Phil has never worked a steady job that didn't involve deceit towards others. He says that he can do whatever he needs to do to survive, and that the law doesn't apply to him because it's about survival. Phil becomes angry when he shares how his wife left with their son, and says he hasn't heard from them in four years. Phil continues to talk, and tells you that he's been in and out of jail since he was 14 years-old; stealing, lying, running away several times, and having sex with any girl he wanted.

What is Phil's presenting problem?

What are the presenting symptoms?

What is the duration?

What is Phil's behavior?

What is Phil's diagnosis?

JoJo is a five-year-old boy who attends kindergarten. Jojo is the youngest child in his family. Claire, Jojo's mom, has been having a hard time with him when it is time to go to school. Jojo has been crying at school and not participating in classroom activities. The teacher has stated that it takes Jojo about two hours to calm down, and once he's calm, he participates in the class activities and interacts with the other children. Claire seeks counseling as she's not sure how to help Jojo. Claire meets with you and tells you that for the last five weeks, Jojo seems stressed whenever he has to go to school. Jojo has been complaining about stomach-aches, and because of this, he can't eat his lunch. Claire has also noticed that Jojo is stressed when she drops him of at play dates and swimming class. Claire has to stay nearby to make sure he's okay and doesn't have a meltdown.

What is JoJo's presenting problem?

What are the presenting symptoms?

What is the duration?

What is JoJo's behavior?

What is JoJo's diagnosis?

Flora is a 48-year-old manager of a mid-sized computer store. Flora is married and has three kids, ages 14, 16, and 19. Flora's oldest son, Ryan, is a freshman in college. Jim is the youngest in the family. At the beginning of the school year, Jim was happy with his friends, enjoying his club activities, and having fun. Recently, Jim seems to be struggling in school. Over the last three weeks, Jim has withdrawn socially and lost interest in the clubs at school. Jim has been experiencing feelings he can't understand. He has feelings of sadness, low self-esteem, and is sometimes unable to concentrate. Flora has noticed that at times, Jim is extremely talkative, impulsive, and easily distracted. Jim tells his mom he has been experiencing these moods since he was about ten years old. Jim further explains that he never said anything about it because he could always handle these moods, and they didn't affect his life. Jim and Flora talk about possible solutions that will help him, but Flora is unsure how to handle this so she seeks a therapist to help her. Flora meets with you.

What is Jim's presenting problem?

What are the presenting symptoms?

What is the duration?

What is Jim's behavior?

What is Jim's diagnosis?

Penny is a four-year-old girl who has been experiencing anxiety when she is around groups of kids. Penny's mom, Joyce, has spoken to her preschool teacher and has tried to come with ways to help Penny. Penny will sit alone in school while other kids try to communicate with her and include her in activities. Penny listens and follows directions from her teachers, and will speak to them when she needs something, but she won't speak to the kids in class. Claire has taken Penny to the doctor and found that Penny is in good health. Penny's pediatrician refers you to a therapist.

What is Penny's presenting problem?

What are the presenting symptoms?

What is the duration?

What is Penny's behavior?

What is Penny's diagnosis?

Case Answers

Jorie	Borderline Personality Disorder	Margo	Anorexia Nervosa
Kyle	Bipolar II	Sophie	Generalized Anxiety Disorder
Carlos	Schizotypal Disorder	Max	Oppositional Defiant Disorder
Jacob	Adjustment Disorder	James	Persistent Depressive Disorder
Jenna	Panic Disorder	Sal	Post Traumatic Stress Disorder
Janet	Billy is the identified client Dependent disorder	Gabby	Substance Abuse Disorder
Anthony	Bipolar I	Doug	Narcissistic Personality Disorder
Ms. Shane	Major Depressive Disorder	Jill	Gender Dysphoria
Lucy	Delusional Disorder	Liza	Histrionic Personality Disorder
Edmond	Schizotypal	Don	Paranoid Personality Disorder
Tara	Oppositional Defiant Disorder	Phil	Anti Social Personality Disorder
Thomas	Disruptive Mood Dysregulation Disorder	JoJo	Separation Anxiety Disorder
Marcus	Conduct Disorder	Jim	Cyclothymic Disorder
Cheryl	Obsessive Compulsive Personality Disorder	Penny	Selective Mutism

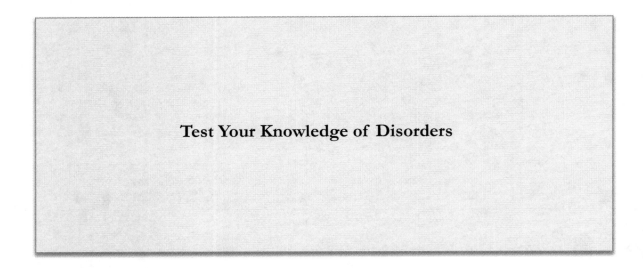

Test Your Knowledge of Disorders

Test your knowledge: Write down the differences

Delusional Disorder	Social Anxiety Disorder	Paranoid Personality Disorder

Duration

Symptoms

Test your knowledge: Fill in the symptoms

Separation Anxiety Disorder	Dependent Personality Disorder	Social Anxiety Disorder

Appears_____	Appears_____	Appears_____
The individual experiences excessive anxiety when separated from an individual to whom they are attached.	Persistent dependence on other people - manifests itself by early adulthood.	Persistent fear of social situations or a situation when the individual may need to perform.

Separation Anxiety Disorder	Dependent Personality Disorder	Social Anxiety Disorder
1. Extreme distress _____ _____ 2. Persistent fear _____ _____ 3. Frequent physical _____ _____	1. The need_____ 2. Inability _____ 3. Relies_____ 4. Relies_____ _____ 5. Difficulties_____ 6. Fear_____ _____ 7. Feeling _____ _____	1. Meeting_____ _____ 2. Easily _____ 3. Feeling _____ 4. Having _____ 5. Being_____ _____ 6. Being_____ _____

Test your knowledge: Write down the differences

Acute Stress Disorder	Adjustment Disorder	Post Traumatic Stress Disorder
Duration	Duration	Duration

Symptoms

Test your knowledge: List the symptoms

Communication Disorders	Learning Disorders	Motor Disorders
Disorders that affect the ability to apply language and speech with other individuals.	Interferes with an individual's ability to learn basic skills: reading, writing, and math.	Involves coordination disorders, stereotypic movement disorder, and tic disorder (formerly Tourette's Disorder).
Symptoms:	Common disabilities include:	Coordination Disorder
		Stereotypic Movement Disorder (symptoms are repetitive and excessive)
Fluency disorder (stuttering)	Symptoms:	Tourette's Disorder
Language disorder		Persistent vocal or motor tic disorders include:

Test your knowledge: List the symptoms

Postpartum Depression

(specifer within Major Depressive Disorder)

A form of depression experienced by women after childbirth. Symptoms can start within the first few weeks of childbirth or months after childbirth. Depressive symptoms, sadness, can interfere with a woman's ability to care for her family and herself. The likelihood of experiencing postpartum depression is higher for women with a history of depression.

Common symptoms include:

Test your knowledge. Fill in the symptoms below:

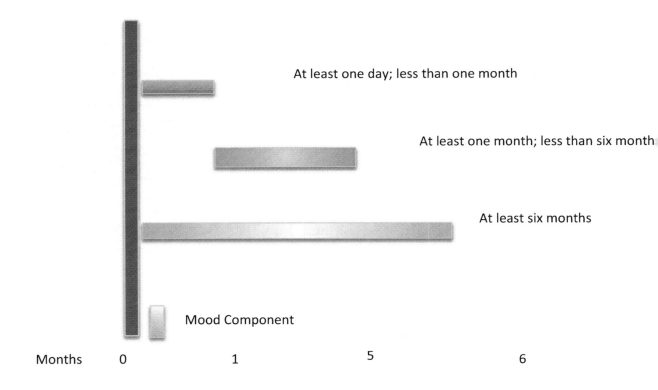

At least one day; less than one month

At least one month; less than six month

At least six months

Mood Component

Months   0   1   5   6

Schizoaffective	Schizophrenia	Schizophreniform	Brief Psychotic Disorder
*Two or more symptoms	*Two or more symptoms	*One or more symptoms	Mood Component

Test your knowledge: List symptoms

Bipolar II

A disorder characterized by a pattern of one or more major depressive episodes and at least one hypomanic episode.

Depressive episode never severe enough to cause impairment in functioning, or to require hospitalization. Symptoms last four days.

Challenge question: What is the difference between Bipolar I & Bipolar II?

Test your knowledge: List symptoms, key difference

Panic Disorder	Generalized Anxiety Disorder

Key Differences ← →

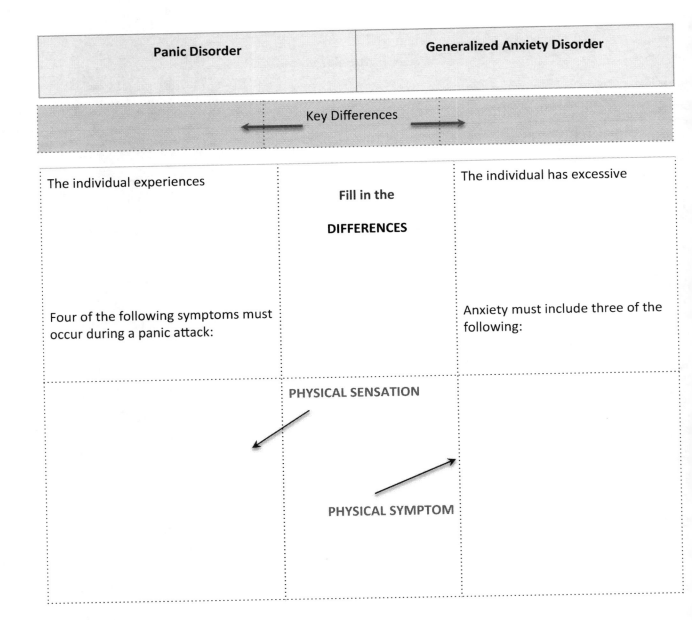

The individual experiences

Fill in the

DIFFERENCES

The individual has excessive

Four of the following symptoms must occur during a panic attack:

Anxiety must include three of the following:

PHYSICAL SENSATION

PHYSICAL SYMPTOM

Test your knowledge: Write down the disorder and symptoms

Key differences

A mental condition – includes impulsive behavior and reckless behavior, unstable relationships and moods. Suffer BRIEF PSYCHOTIC mood swings.	Individual is vulnerable (emotionally) and needs constant praise from people. Inappropriately seductive, manipulative, and flirtatious.	Individual has a significantly inflated sense of self-worth. Lacks empathy, has an arrogant attitude, is envious, and exploits other individuals.

Test your knowledge: Write down the symptoms

Insomnia	Non-Rapid Eye Movement Arousal
When an individual has difficulty falling asleep and/or staying asleep. Starts in young adulthood.	Individual's brain is partially awake and partly in REM sleep.

Test your knowledge: Write down the symptoms and duration

Intermittent Explosive Disorder

(Late Childhood - Adolescence)

This disorder involves repeated, sudden episodes of impulsive, aggressive, and/or angry verbal outbursts, in which the individual reacts disproportionately to the situation.

Test your knowledge: Write down the symptoms

Disruptive Mood Dysregulation Disorder

(Children - Teenagers)

This disorder involves persistent, irritable, or angry moods and frequent temper outbursts that are disproportionate to the situation. Similar to ODD and Bipolar.

Test your knowledge: Write down the symptoms

Factious Disorder	An individual intentionally manifests physical or psychological symptoms in order to satisfy the need to fill the role of a sick person:
Illness Anxiety Disorder	A preoccupation with having or getting a serious illness (formerly hypochondriasis). Symptoms must be present for six months:
Malingering Disorder	Physical symptoms to avoid a specific activity, such as going to work or receiving an award:
Conversion Disorder	The loss of bodily function; serious physical disease:
Somatic Symptom Disorder	Individual may suggest a medical condition exists but isn't explainable:

Test your knowledge: Write down the symptoms

Obsessive Compulsive Disorder	Obsessive Compulsive Personality Disorder

Key Difference

OCD is an ANXIETY disorder. Presence of true OBSESSION and/or COMPULSION.	OCPD is STRICT ADHERENCE to orderliness and control over one's environment at the expense of flexibility to new experiences.

Write Your Own Case

In this section, you will come up with information about a client.

The goal is to learn about your client, the presenting problem, symptoms, and effects of the symptoms so that you can formulate a diagnosis to treat your client.

Test your knowledge: Write a case for the following disorder

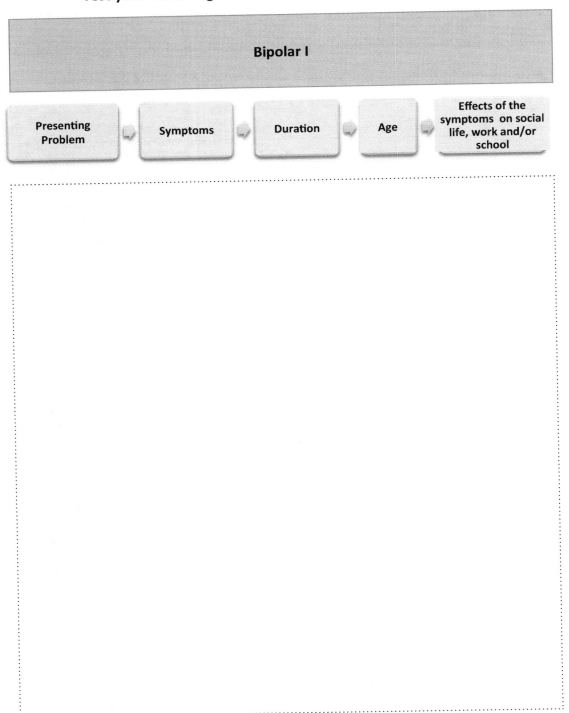

Test your knowledge: Write a case for the following disorder

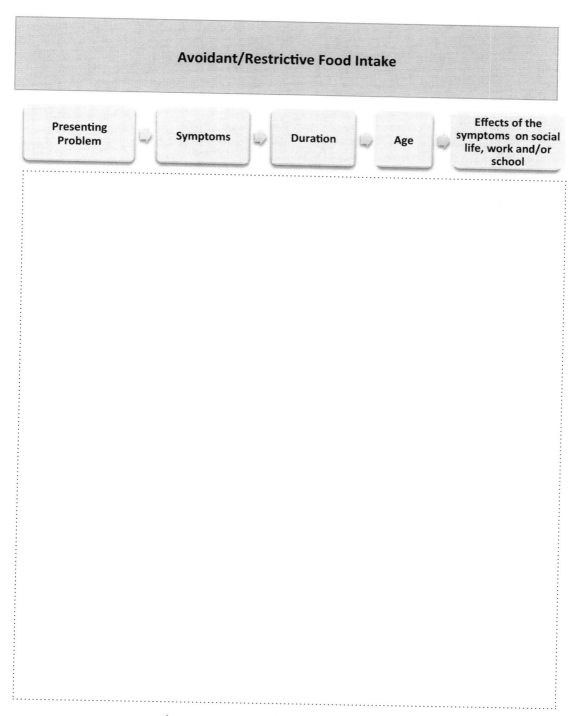

Avoidant/Restrictive Food Intake

Presenting Problem	Symptoms	Duration	Age	Effects of the symptoms on social life, work and/or school

Test your knowledge: Write a case for the following disorder

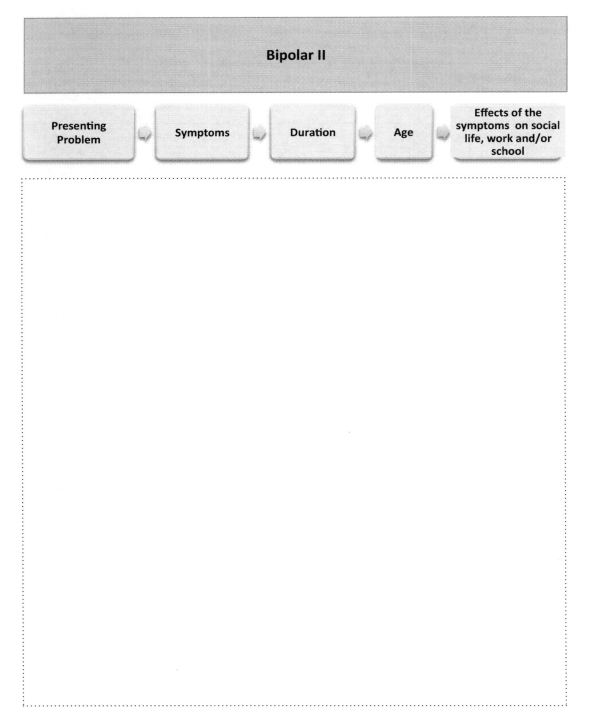

Bipolar II

| Presenting Problem | Symptoms | Duration | Age | Effects of the symptoms on social life, work and/or school |

Test your knowledge: Write a case for the following disorder

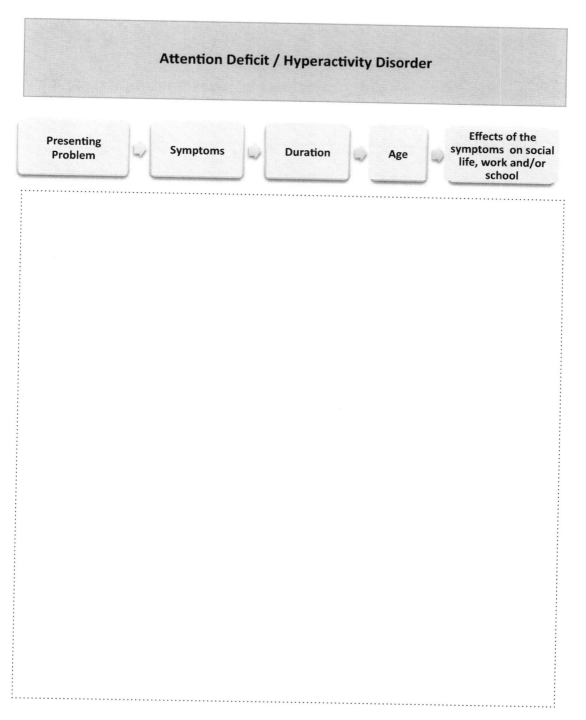

Attention Deficit / Hyperactivity Disorder

| Presenting Problem | Symptoms | Duration | Age | Effects of the symptoms on social life, work and/or school |

Test your knowledge: Write a case for the following disorder

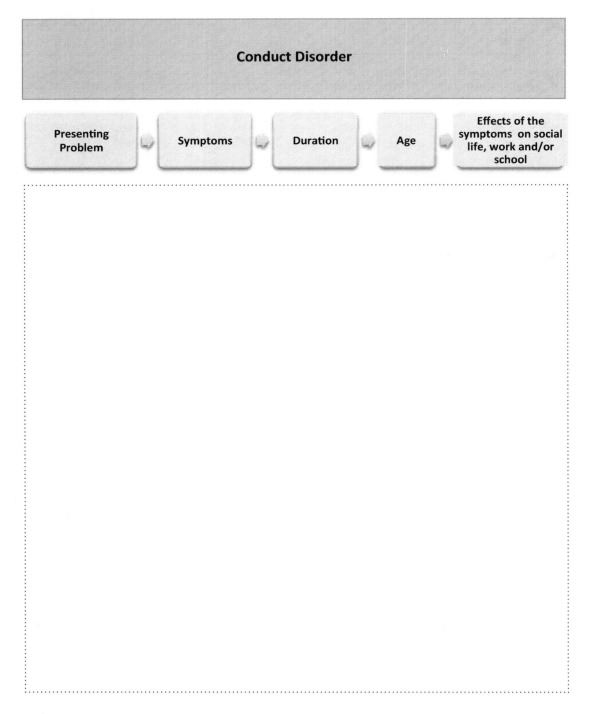

Conduct Disorder

| Presenting Problem | Symptoms | Duration | Age | Effects of the symptoms on social life, work and/or school |

Test your knowledge: Write a case for the following disorder

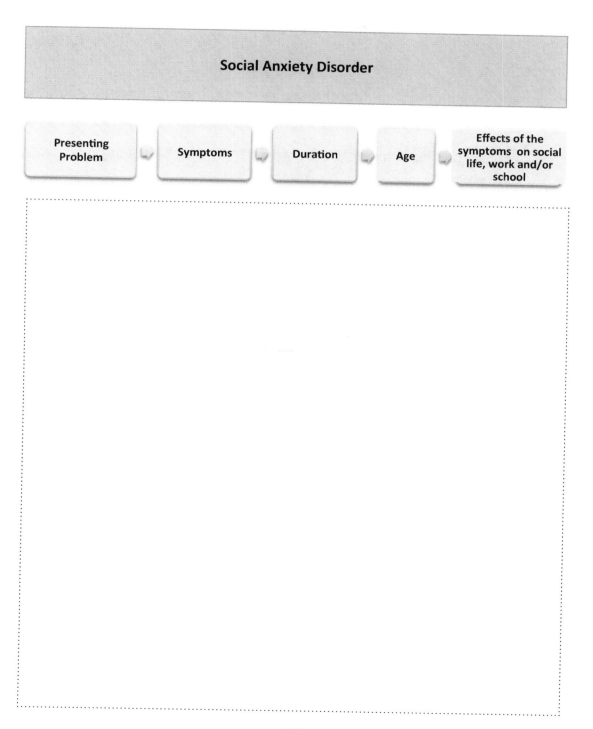

Test your knowledge: Write a case for the following disorder

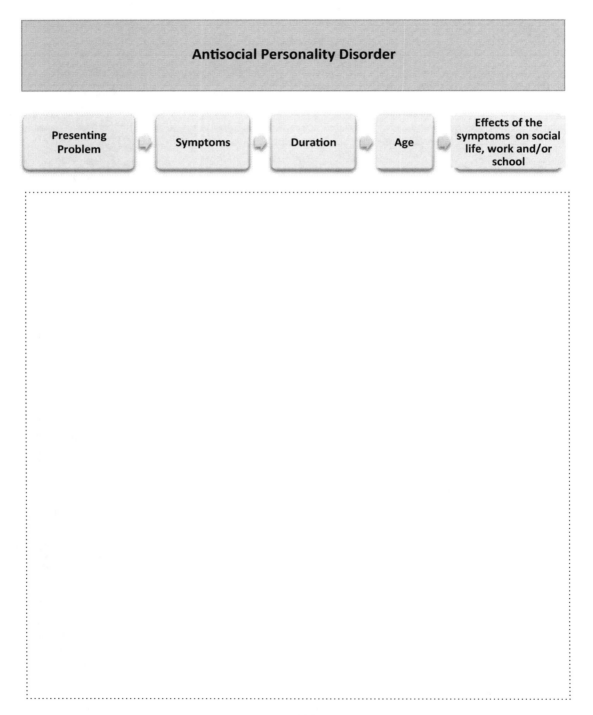

Antisocial Personality Disorder

| Presenting Problem | Symptoms | Duration | Age | Effects of the symptoms on social life, work and/or school |

Test your knowledge: Write a case for the following disorder

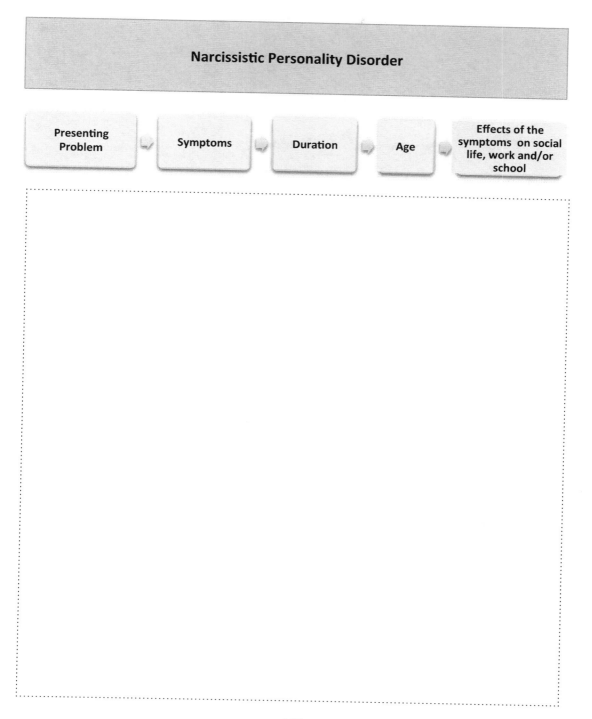

Narcissistic Personality Disorder

| Presenting Problem | Symptoms | Duration | Age | Effects of the symptoms on social life, work and/or school |

Test your knowledge: Write a case for the following disorder

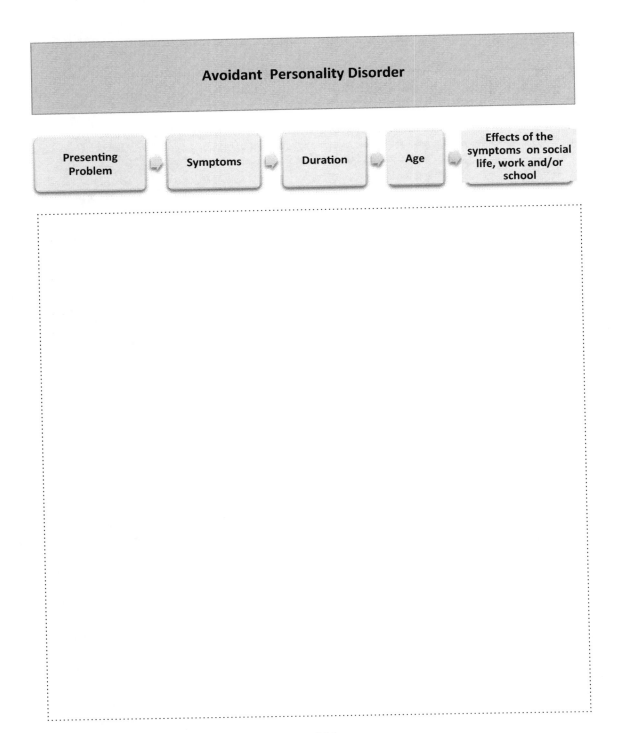

Test your knowledge: Write a case for the following disorder

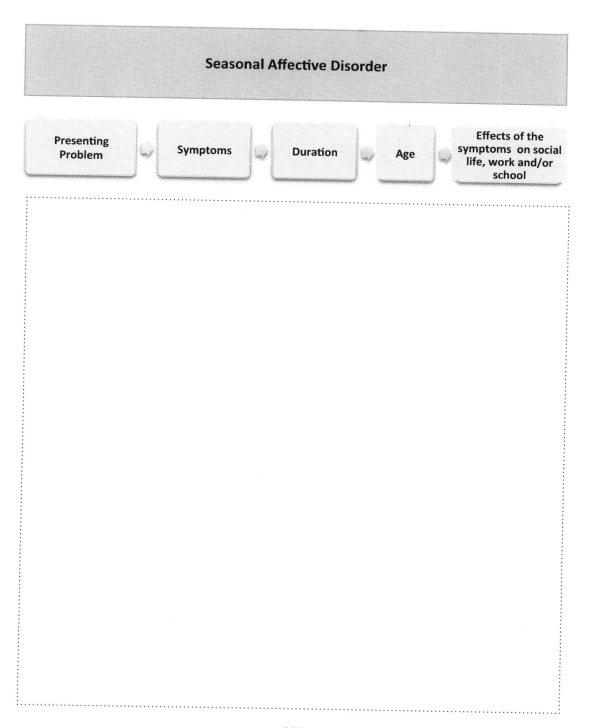

Test your knowledge: Write a case for the following disorder

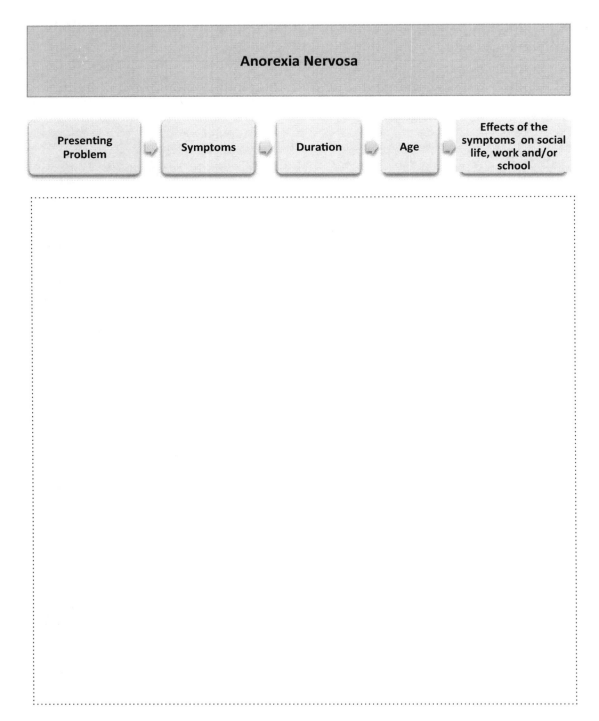

Anorexia Nervosa

| Presenting Problem | Symptoms | Duration | Age | Effects of the symptoms on social life, work and/or school |

Test your knowledge: Write a case for the following disorder

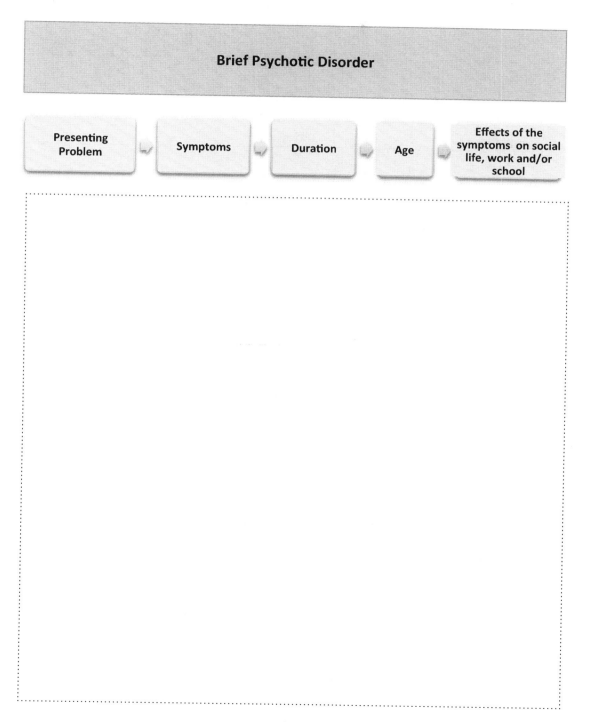

Brief Psychotic Disorder

Presenting Problem → Symptoms → Duration → Age → Effects of the symptoms on social life, work and/or school

Test your knowledge: Write a case for the following disorder

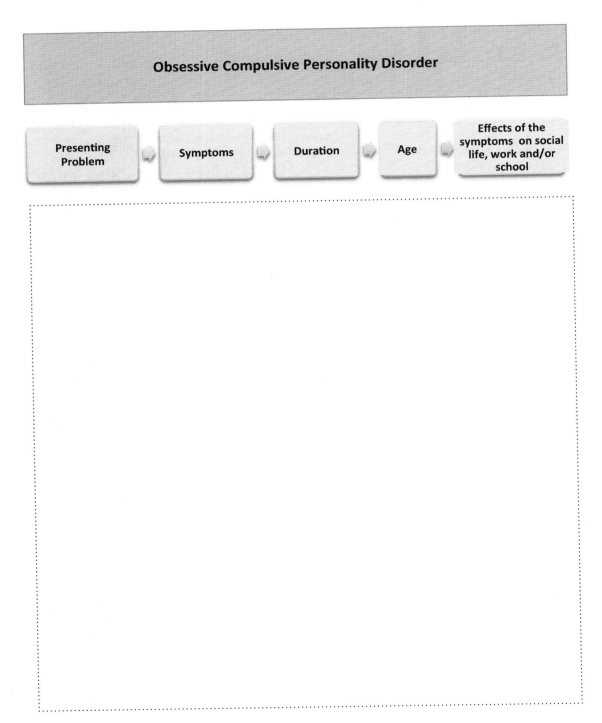

| Obsessive Compulsive Personality Disorder |

| Presenting Problem | Symptoms | Duration | Age | Effects of the symptoms on social life, work and/or school |

Test your knowledge: Write a case for the following disorder

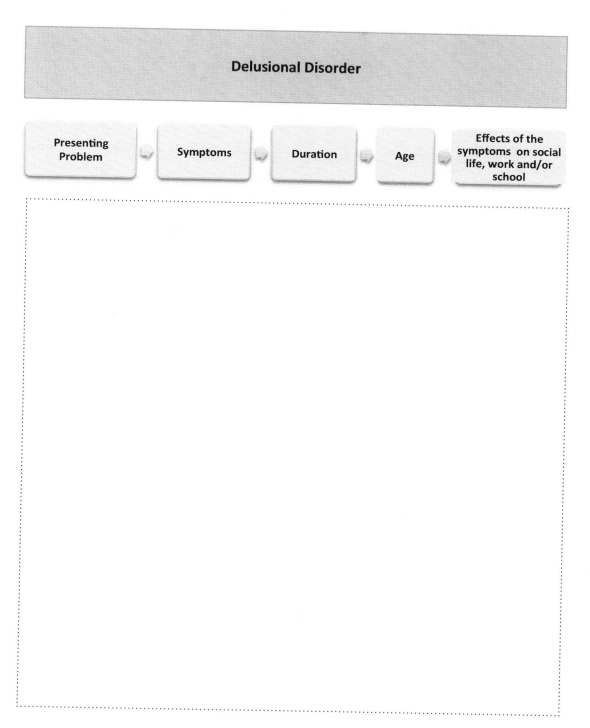

Delusional Disorder

Presenting Problem → Symptoms → Duration → Age → Effects of the symptoms on social life, work and/or school

Test your knowledge: Write a case for the following disorder

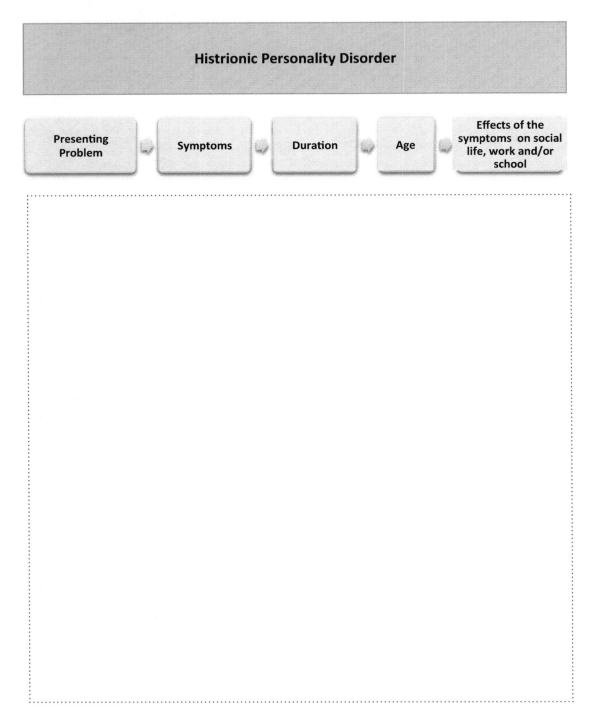

Histrionic Personality Disorder

| Presenting Problem | Symptoms | Duration | Age | Effects of the symptoms on social life, work and/or school |

Test your knowledge: Write a case for the following disorder

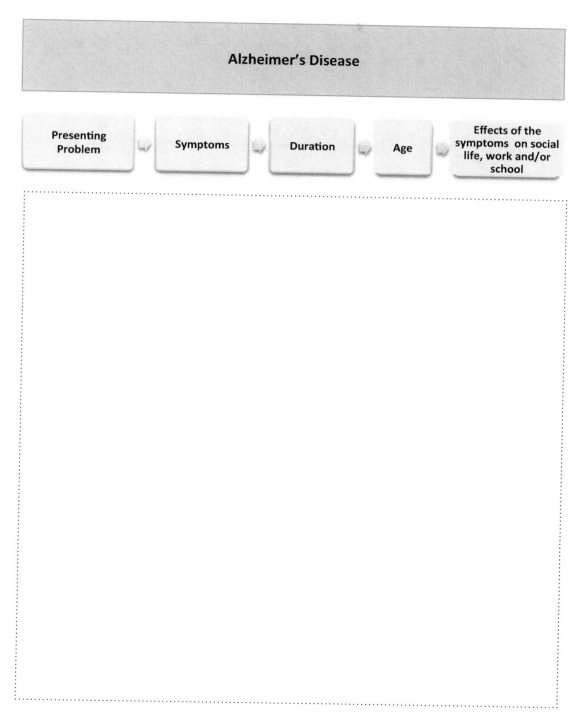

Alzheimer's Disease

| Presenting Problem | Symptoms | Duration | Age | Effects of the symptoms on social life, work and/or school |

Test your knowledge: Write a case for the following disorder

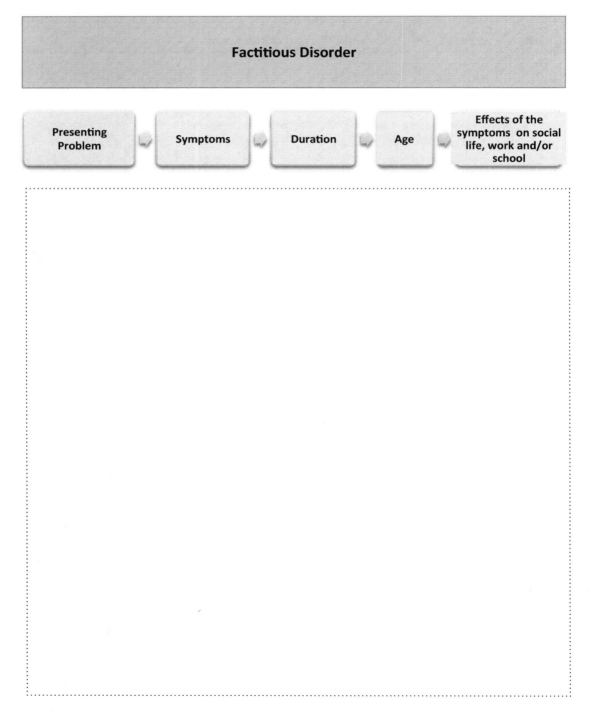

Factitious Disorder

Presenting Problem → Symptoms → Duration → Age → Effects of the symptoms on social life, work and/or school

Test your knowledge: Write a case for the following disorder

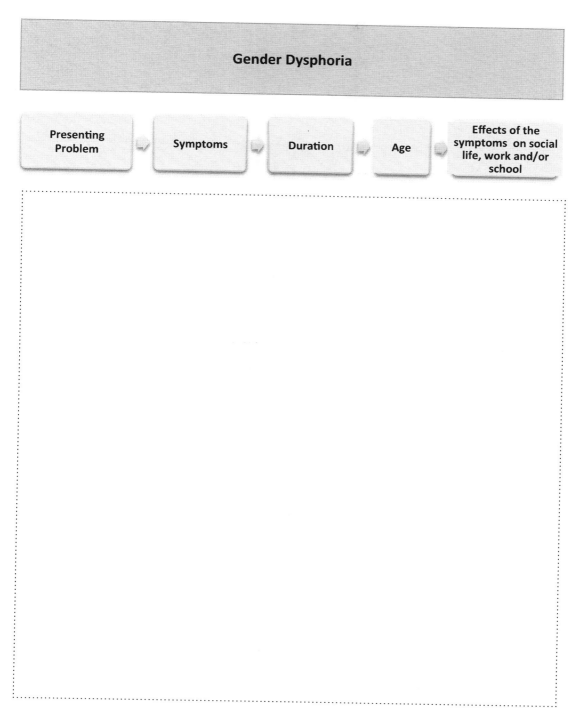

Gender Dysphoria

Presenting Problem → Symptoms → Duration → Age → Effects of the symptoms on social life, work and/or school

Test your knowledge: Write a case for the following disorder

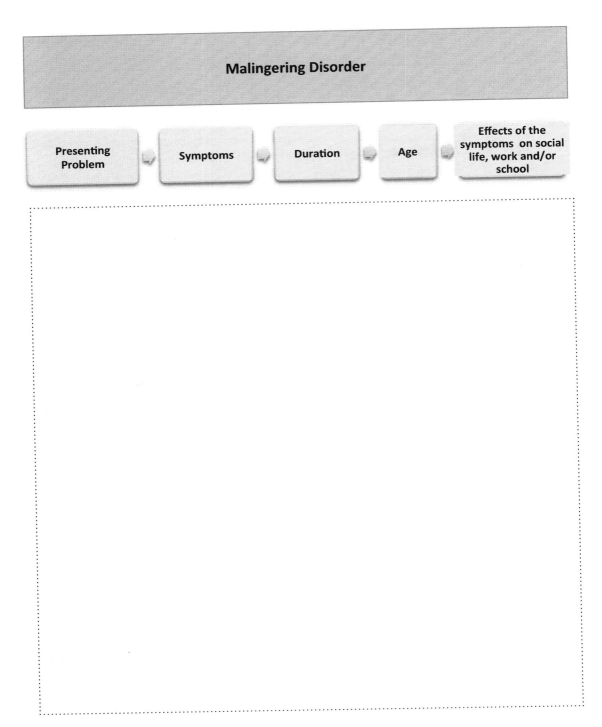

Test your knowledge: Write a case for the following disorder

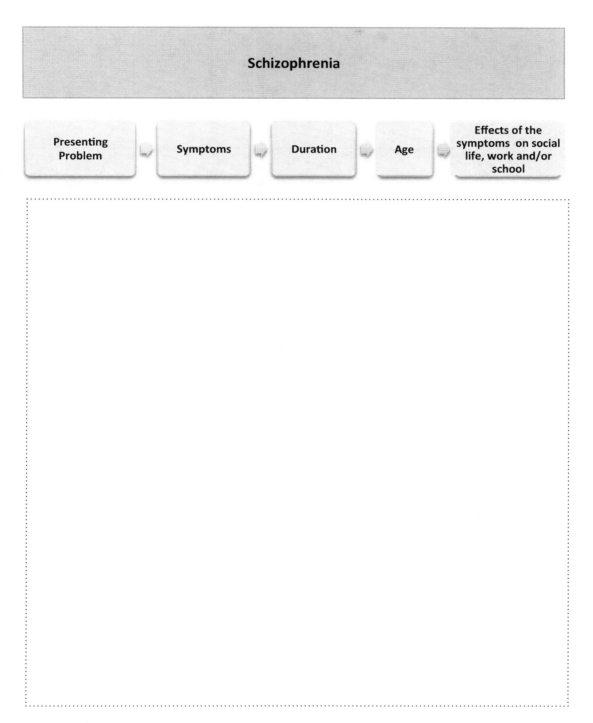

Schizophrenia

| Presenting Problem | Symptoms | Duration | Age | Effects of the symptoms on social life, work and/or school |

Test your knowledge: Write a case for the following disorder

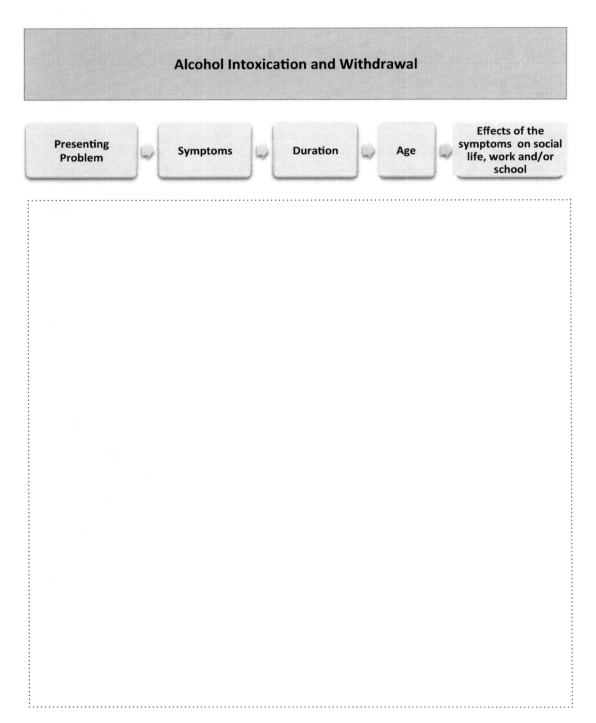

Alcohol Intoxication and Withdrawal

Presenting Problem	Symptoms	Duration	Age	Effects of the symptoms on social life, work and/or school

Test your knowledge: Write a case for the following disorder

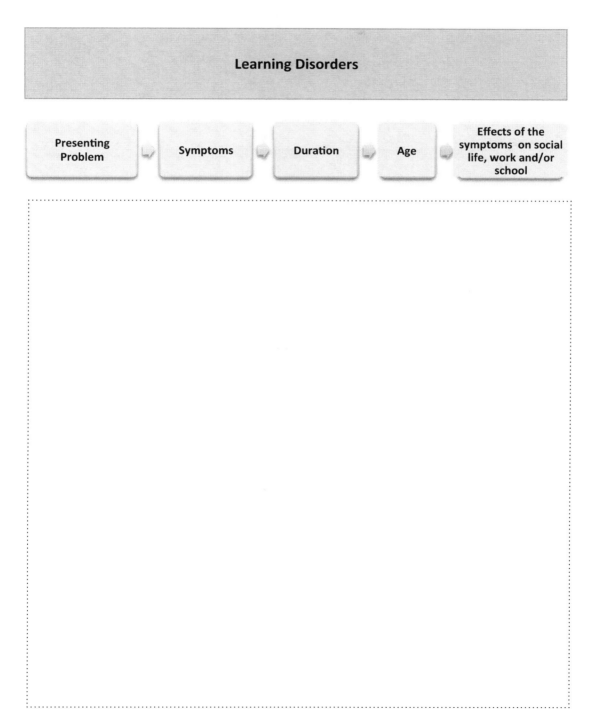

Learning Disorders				
Presenting Problem	Symptoms	Duration	Age	Effects of the symptoms on social life, work and/or school

Test your knowledge: Write a case for the following disorder

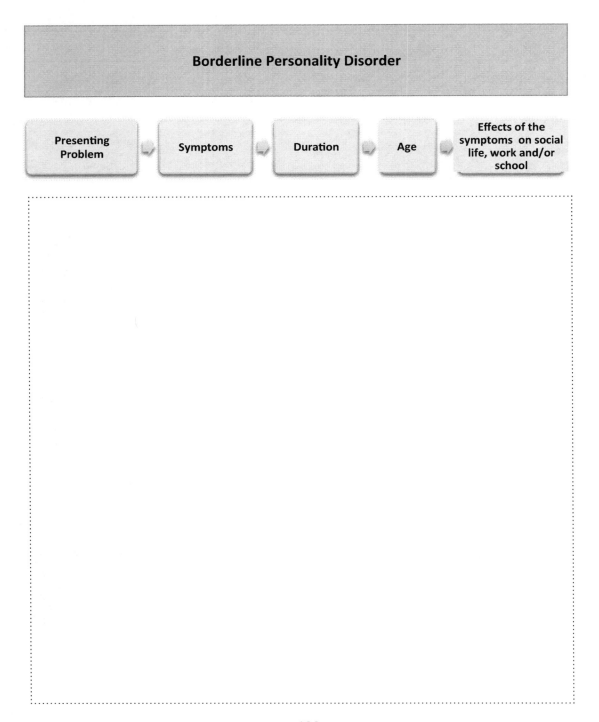

Borderline Personality Disorder

Presenting Problem → Symptoms → Duration → Age → Effects of the symptoms on social life, work and/or school

Test your knowledge: Write a case for the following disorder

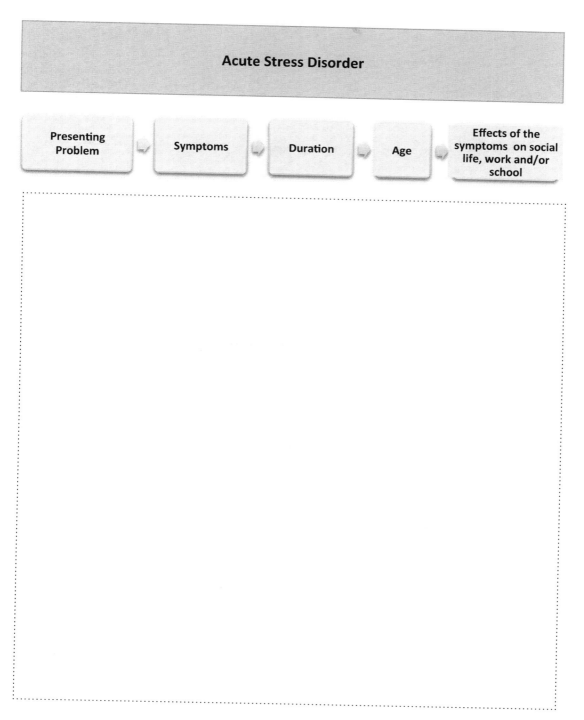

Acute Stress Disorder

| Presenting Problem | Symptoms | Duration | Age | Effects of the symptoms on social life, work and/or school |

Test your knowledge: Write a case for the following disorder

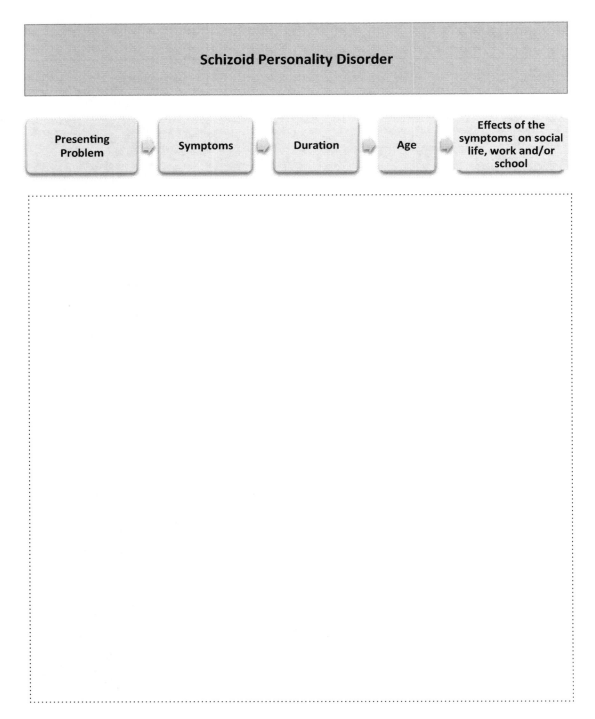

Test your knowledge: Write a case for the following disorder

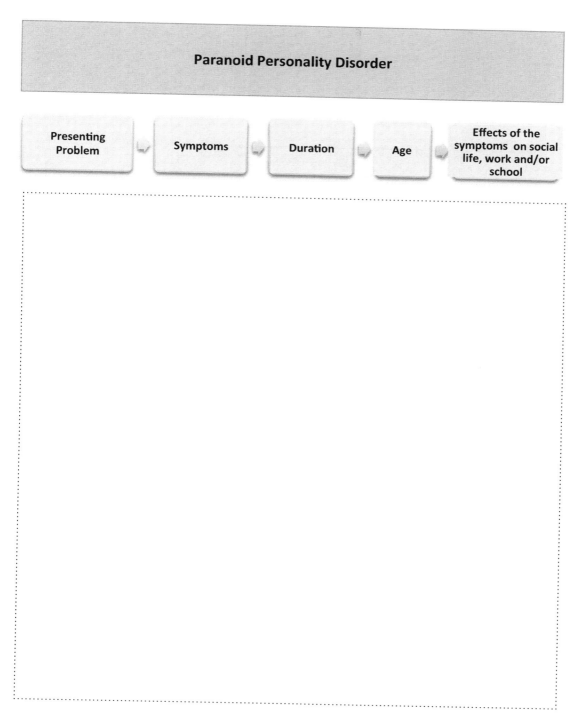

Paranoid Personality Disorder

Presenting Problem → Symptoms → Duration → Age → Effects of the symptoms on social life, work and/or school

Test your knowledge: Write a case for the following disorder

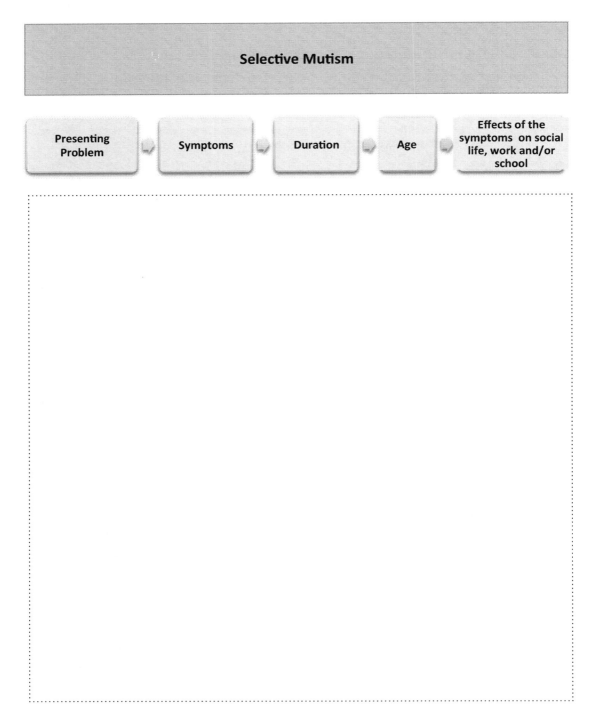

Selective Mutism

Presenting Problem	Symptoms	Duration	Age	Effects of the symptoms on social life, work and/or school

Test your knowledge: Write a case for the following disorder

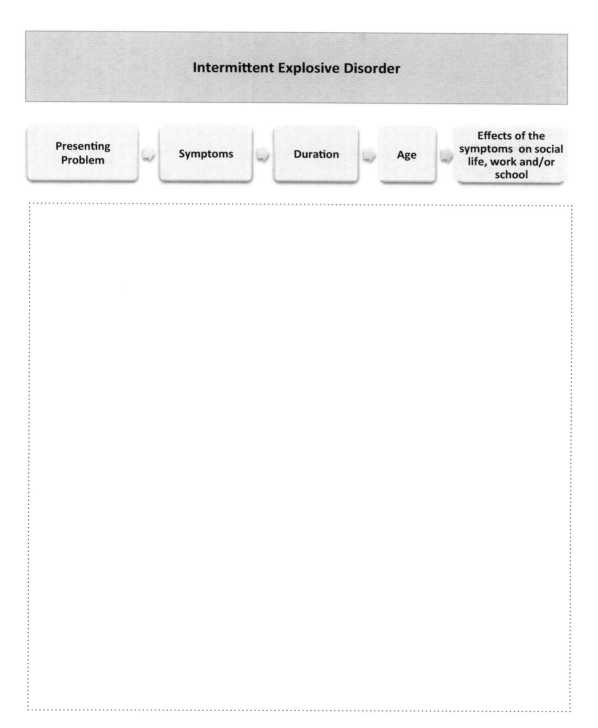

Intermittent Explosive Disorder

Presenting Problem → Symptoms → Duration → Age → Effects of the symptoms on social life, work and/or school

Test your knowledge: Write a case for the following disorder

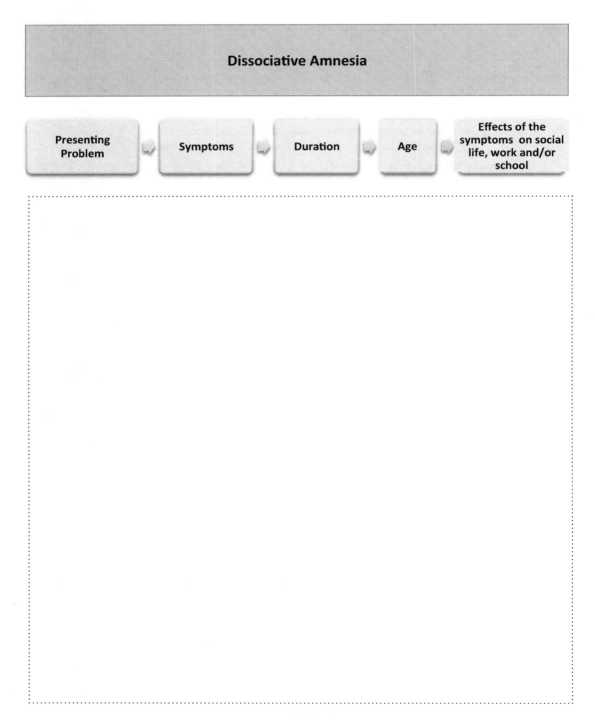

Dissociative Amnesia

| Presenting Problem | Symptoms | Duration | Age | Effects of the symptoms on social life, work and/or school |

Test your knowledge: Write a case for the following disorder

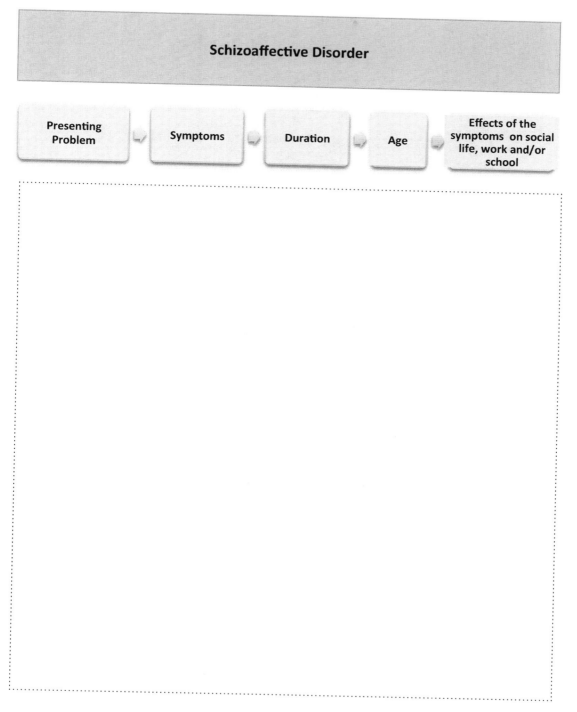

Schizoaffective Disorder

| Presenting Problem | Symptoms | Duration | Age | Effects of the symptoms on social life, work and/or school |

Test your knowledge: Write a case for the following disorder

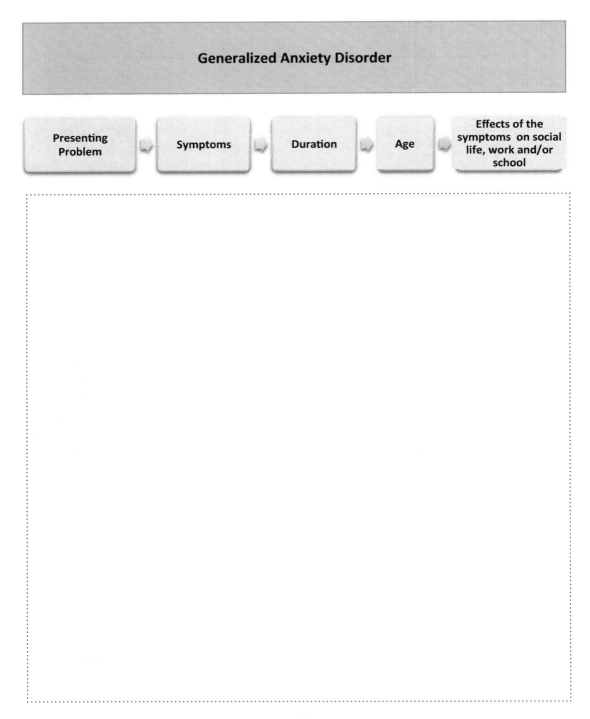

Generalized Anxiety Disorder

| Presenting Problem | Symptoms | Duration | Age | Effects of the symptoms on social life, work and/or school |

Test your knowledge: Write a case for the following disorder

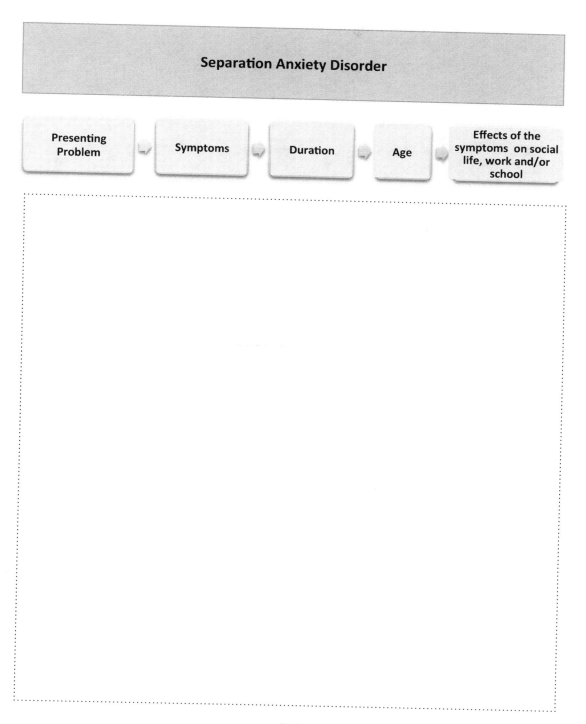

Separation Anxiety Disorder

| Presenting Problem | Symptoms | Duration | Age | Effects of the symptoms on social life, work and/or school |

Test your knowledge: Write a case for the following disorder

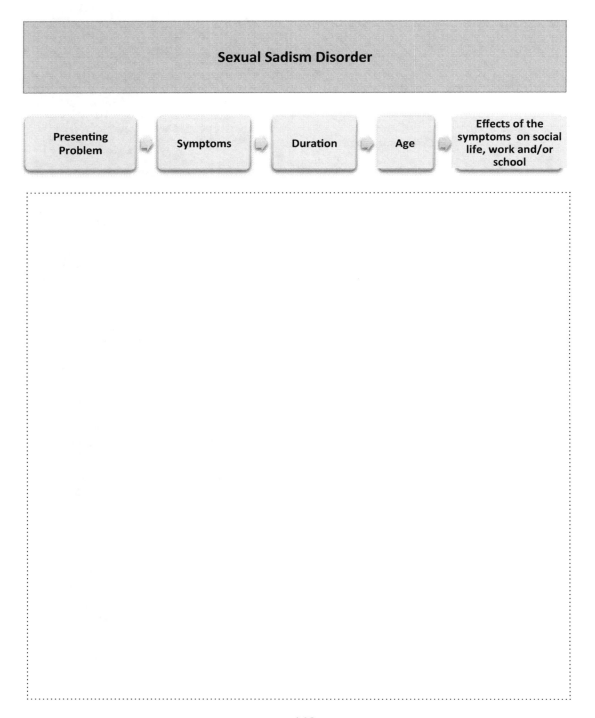

Sexual Sadism Disorder

Presenting Problem → Symptoms → Duration → Age → Effects of the symptoms on social life, work and/or school

Test your knowledge: Write a case for the following disorder

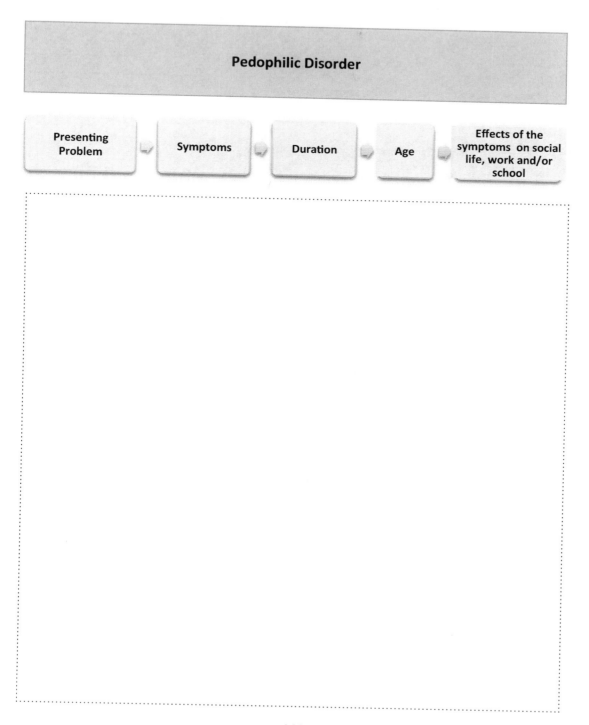

Pedophilic Disorder

Presenting Problem → Symptoms → Duration → Age → Effects of the symptoms on social life, work and/or school

Test your knowledge: Write a case for the following disorder

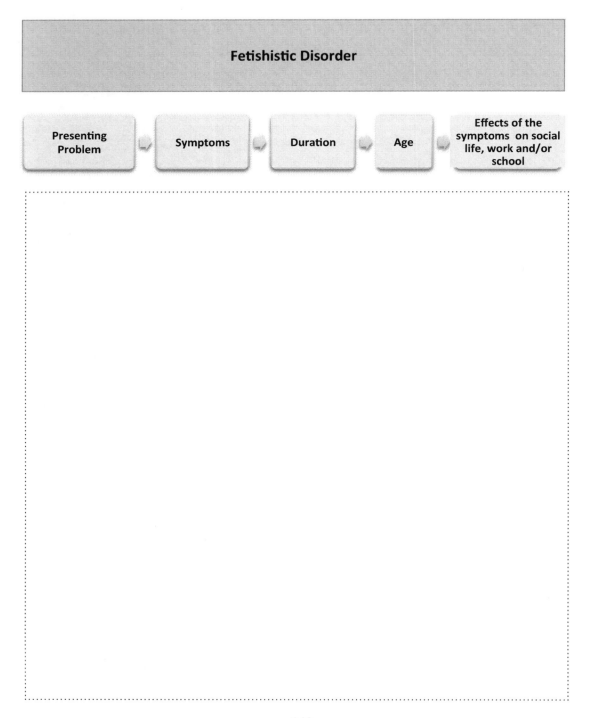

Fetishistic Disorder

Presenting Problem	Symptoms	Duration	Age	Effects of the symptoms on social life, work and/or school

Test your knowledge: Write a case for the following disorder

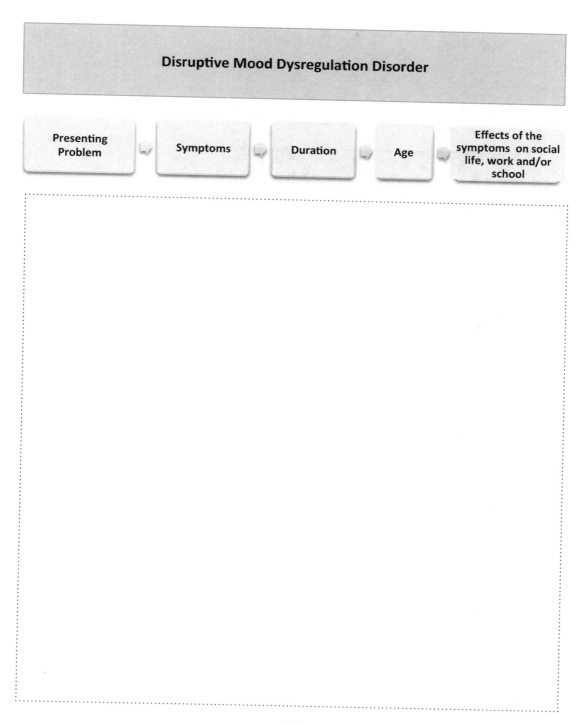

Disruptive Mood Dysregulation Disorder

| Presenting Problem | Symptoms | Duration | Age | Effects of the symptoms on social life, work and/or school |

Test your knowledge: Write a case for the following disorder

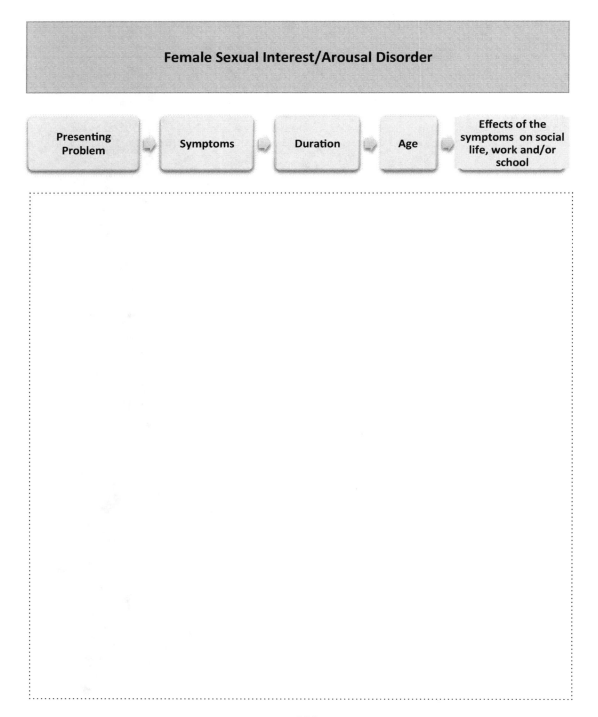

Female Sexual Interest/Arousal Disorder

| Presenting Problem | Symptoms | Duration | Age | Effects of the symptoms on social life, work and/or school |

Test your knowledge: Write a case for the following disorder

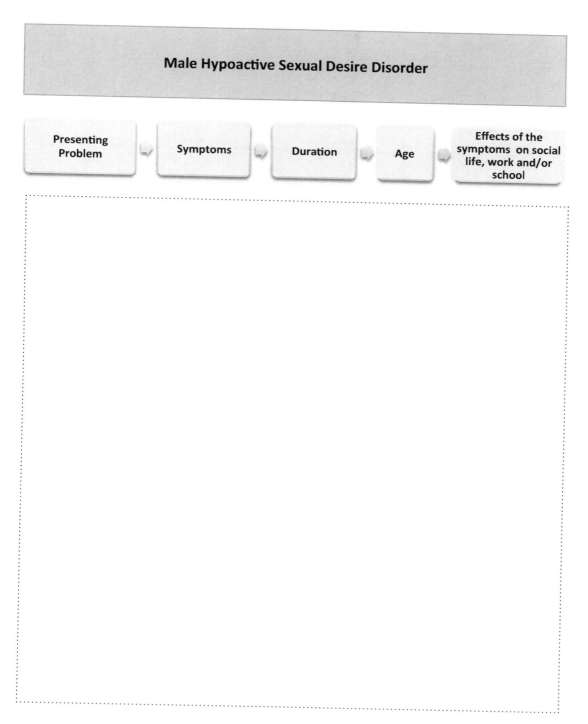

Male Hypoactive Sexual Desire Disorder

Presenting Problem → Symptoms → Duration → Age → Effects of the symptoms on social life, work and/or school

Practice: STEP 1. Think of an individual. It could be a friend, a random person, or even yourself. STEP 2. Each leaf you place on this tree will represent a symptom of their disorder. STEP 3. The severe symptoms will be closer to the top of the tree and the less severe symptoms will be closer to the bottom. STEP 4. Make it interesting; use colored pens or pencils to distinguish severity/symptoms/duration. STEP 5. Once completed, think about the following: How does the tree look and feel to you? How does the tree make you feel? How do you see the disorder you've chosen? STEP 6. Optional: Did this exercise help you better understand the disorder?

Adjustment Disorders

Adjustment Disorders
Anxiety Disorder
Binge Eating Disorder
Bipolar Disorder
Gender Dysphoria
Histrionic Personality Disorder
Narcissistic Personality Disorder
Obsessive Compulsive Disorder
Panic Disorder
PTSD
Postpartum Disorder
Seasonal Affective Disorder
Rett's Disorder
Separation Anxiety Disorder
Sleepwalking Disorder

Anxiety Disorders

Acute Stress Disorder
Adjustment Disorder
Agoraphobia
Alzheimer's
Antisocial Personality Disorder
Anxiety Disorder
Borderline Personality
Dependent Personality
Generalized Anxiety
Hypochondriasis
Intermittent Explosive
Narcolepsy
Obsessive Compulsive
Obsessive Compulsive Personality
Panic Disorder
Paranoid Personality
PTSD
Selective Mutism
Separation anxiety
Sexual Dysfunction
Social Anxiety

Cognitive Disorders

Alzheimer's Disease
Attention Deficit Hyperactivity Disorder
Breathing Related Sleep Disorder
Dissociative Amnesia
Dissociative Disorder
Learning Disorders
Parkinson's Disease

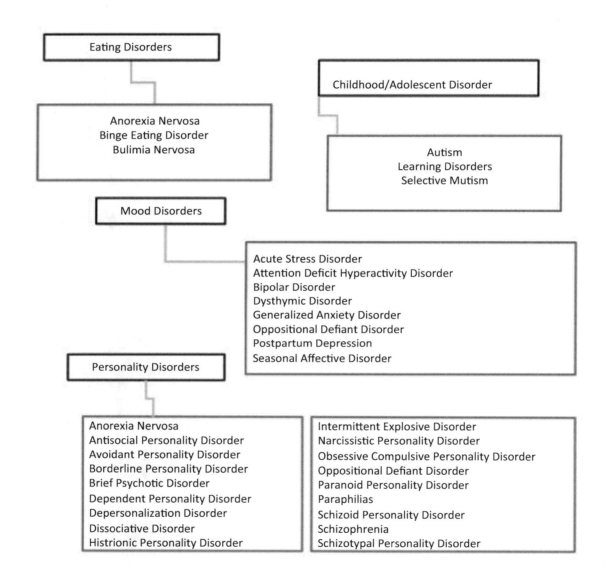

Eating Disorders

Anorexia Nervosa
Binge Eating Disorder
Bulimia Nervosa

Childhood/Adolescent Disorder

Autism
Learning Disorders
Selective Mutism

Mood Disorders

Acute Stress Disorder
Attention Deficit Hyperactivity Disorder
Bipolar Disorder
Dysthymic Disorder
Generalized Anxiety Disorder
Oppositional Defiant Disorder
Postpartum Depression
Seasonal Affective Disorder

Personality Disorders

Anorexia Nervosa
Antisocial Personality Disorder
Avoidant Personality Disorder
Borderline Personality Disorder
Brief Psychotic Disorder
Dependent Personality Disorder
Depersonalization Disorder
Dissociative Disorder
Histrionic Personality Disorder

Intermittent Explosive Disorder
Narcissistic Personality Disorder
Obsessive Compulsive Personality Disorder
Oppositional Defiant Disorder
Paranoid Personality Disorder
Paraphilias
Schizoid Personality Disorder
Schizophrenia
Schizotypal Personality Disorder

References

American Psychiatric Association, Diagnostic and Statistical Manual for Mental Disorders, DSM-5 (2013) APA Press 5th Edition

Corcoran & Fisher, (2000). *Measures for Clinical Practice*: A Sourcebook. 3rd Edition. Free Press

Corey, G (2017). *Theory and Practice of Counseling and Psychotherapy*. Boston, MA: Cengage Learning

Curran, L. A. (2013). *101 trauma-informed interventions: Activities, exercises and assignments for moving the client and therapy forward*. Eau Claire, WI: PESI

Drummond, R. Jones, K. (2009). *Assessment Procedures for Counselors and Helping Professionals*, 7th Edition. Prentice Hall

Gabbard, G.O., (2014). *Treatments of Psychiatric Disorders*, 3rd Edition, vol. 1 & 2. Washington, DC. American Psychiatric Press

Marcusston, D. W., & Marcusston, M. (2001). *Comprehensive clinical psychology*. Amsterdam: Elsevier

Kress, V.E., & Paylo, M.J. (2014), *Treating those with mental disorders; A comprehensive approach to case conceptualization and treatment*. New York, NY: Pearson

Neukrug, E., & Fawcet, R.C. (2015). *Essentials of Testing and Assessment*: A practical guide to counselors, social workers, and psychologists. Stamford, CT: Cengage Learning

Reichenberg, Lourie W., & Seligman, Linda. (2016). *Selecting Effective Treatments*. A comprehensive Systematic Guide to Treating Mental Disorders, Hoboken, NJ: Wiley

Rosenthal, H. (2006). *Therapy's best:* Practical advice and gems of wisdom from twenty accomplished counselors and therapists. New York: Haworth Press

Roth, A., Fonagy, P., (2005), *What Works for Whom?* Second Edition A Critical Review of Psychotherapy Research, NY: Guilford Press

Made in the
USA
Columbia, SC